THE LIFE AND TIMES OF FRANZ ALEXANDER

THE LIFE AND TIMES OF FRANZ ALEXANDER
From Budapest to California

Ilonka Venier Alexander

Routledge
Taylor & Francis Group

LONDON AND NEW YORK

First published 2015 by
Karnac Books Ltd.

Published 2018 by Routledge
2 Park Square, Milton Park, Abingdon, Oxon OX14 4RN
711 Third Avenue, New York, NY 10017, USA

Routledge is an imprint of the Taylor & Francis Group, an informa business

British Library Cataloguing in Publication Data

A C.I.P. for this book is available from the British Library

ISBN-13: 9781782202509 (pbk)

Typeset by V Publishing Solutions Pvt Ltd., Chennai, India

To my good friend Julia Gunn
and Broessler cousins around the World

CONTENTS

ACKNOWLEDGEMENTS

I am grateful to Sandra Phinney, my friend and literary mentor, for her long and persistent encouragement and guidance in the process of writing this book. She never lost faith in the product nor in my ability to get it done.

Once again, I thank my long-time friend, travelling companion, and confidante, Julia Gunn, for her friendship, love, and desire that I find family. Without her, this book and the coming together of family would not have been possible.

I am especially grateful to my literary agent, Arnold Gosewich, for his willingness to take a chance on me, an unknown, when he saw my passion for this work.

This book would not have been possible without the assistance of the staff and members of the Chicago Institute for Psychoanalysis, and the Boston and New York Institutes as well as the American Psychoanalytic Association. Their support and willingness to collaborate during the writing process was immeasurable.

To those, too many to mention, who were part of the research process, either on the phone, in person, or through the internet, a huge thank you. Your participation in this worldwide gathering of information was essential for an honest portrayal of my grandfather. Through our work together much new information was unearthed.

I thank Brian Oram, Nauszika Mathe-Arvay, and Dr. Vera Alexander for their helpful reading of this manuscript. All three provided meaningful suggestions for improvements.

I am indebted to my friend Dr. Imke Kattelmann who wrote her own doctoral thesis about Franz Alexander. She always answered my call for help and, even while on vacation in Japan, assisted with research.

Without the knowledge and genealogical expertise of distant cousin, Raymond Minkus, newly unearthed information about Bernard Alexander's parents and siblings would not have been discovered. Instead, secrets and rumours would have persisted for another hundred years.

Bill Curry's expertise in the field of professional photography is greatly appreciated. Without his time and knowledge, and special equipment, the old photographs could not have been included in the book. They are important and they tell an important part of the story.

I thank Karnac Books for realizing this work has a home on its bookshelves.

And to Graham, my loving husband, thank you for your ongoing support and patience.

ABOUT THE AUTHOR

Ilonka Venier Alexander is a clinical social worker, psychotherapist, and mental health manager with a successful career in the US and Canada. She testified before the United States Congress in the early days of the HIV epidemic about its impact on Boston area veterans during which time her specialization was adults with a severe and persistent mental illness. Later she turned her focus to child and adolescent mental health. She received her Masters of Social Work degree from the University of Southern California and is the granddaughter of Dr. Franz Alexander, founder of the Chicago Institute for Psychoanalysis. She is currently working with her Hungarian cousins to prepare a translation for publication of the diary of her great uncle Artúr Rényi—a unique memoir which documents the fate of the Jews of Hungary during the Nazi regime—as well as a more personal memoir of her life with her grandfather, entitled *Growing up Alexander*.

SERIES EDITOR'S FOREWORD

With the exception of such rare men as Sigmund Freud, Sándor Ferenczi, Ernest Jones and, subsequently, Donald Winnicott, few psychoanalysts have pioneered as many different fields of psychological enquiry as the Hungarian-born clinician, researcher, teacher, author, and administrator Franz Gabriel Alexander.

A man of profound and wide-ranging creativity, Alexander began to publish substantial works before the age of forty, beginning with a monograph—much admired by Freud—entitled *Psychoanalyse der Gesamtpersönlichkeit: Neun Vorlesungen über die Anwendung von Freuds Ichtheorie auf die Neurosenlehre* [*Psychoanalysis of the Total Personality: Nine Lectures on the Application of Freud's Ego Theory to the Study of the Neuroses*] (Alexander, 1927; cf. Alexander, 1926). This groundbreaking text—one of the very first studies of psychoanalytical characterology—inaugurated a profound shift in emphasis from the treatment of discrete symptoms to an understanding of the entire personality structure (cf. Fuechtner, 2011).

Not long thereafter, during the early 1930s, Franz Alexander embarked upon his long-term investigation of the psychological roots of ostensibly physical symptomatology, and in doing so he gradually became the principal architect of the field of psychosomatic medicine. Building upon the earlier work of psychoanalytical figures such as Georg Groddeck (e.g., Will, 1984; cf. Lipsitt, 2000, 2006; Harrington, 2008; Weiner, 2008), Alexander devoted much of his career to primary research on the deep unconscious psychological origins of many bodily symptoms, especially those which had foxed traditional physicians (e.g., Alexander and Szasz, 1952; Alexander, 1957).

Throughout a long lifetime, Alexander succeeded in obtaining funding from the Rockefeller Foundation—perhaps the very first time that a psychoanalyst had received a major research grant—and ultimately, he laid the foundations for understanding the particular aetiological components of various manifestations of illness (Alexander, 1960; Brown, 1987). For instance, Alexander advanced the hypothesis that bronchial asthma might result, in part, from a threat of detachment from the mother, while rheumatoid arthritis might stem from conflicts around aggressive impulses. He made similar contributions to the understanding of such vexing conditions as ulcerative colitis, essential hypertension, neurodermatitis, hypothyroidism, and peptic ulcer (e.g., Alexander, French, and Pollock, 1968), as well as to the understanding of Graves' Disease, which, Alexander and his colleagues had hypothesised, might result from early childhood fears (Ham, Alexander, and Carmichael, 1950).

Of course, other early psychoanalytical researchers had investigated psychosomatic phenomena, most especially Professor Felix Deutsch (e.g., Deutsch, 1953, 1959; Deutsch, Thompson, Pinderhughes, and Goodglass, 1962a, 1962b; cp. Deutsch and Kauf, 1924), as well as Dr. Helen Flanders Dunbar (e.g., Dunbar, 1935, 1943, 1947, 1959; Dunbar Arlow, Hussey, Lewin, Lowe, Rubin, Schneider, and Sontag, 1948) and, also, Professor Roy Grinker (e.g., Grinker and Spiegel, 1943, 1945; Grinker, 1953; cf. Freeman, 1956), and, to a certain extent Dr. Abram Kardiner (Kardiner, 1932, 1941; Kardiner and Spiegel, 1947), but none did so as broadly and as penetratively as Alexander had done. Indeed, when the periodical *Psychosomatic Medicine* began publication in 1939, Alexander (1939a, 1939b, 1939c)—one of the journal's editors—contributed no fewer than three separate articles to the very first issue (Volume 1, Number 1). Although contemporary psychosomaticists have critiqued Alexander's rather linear model of causation, one wonders whether psychosomatic medicine would have flourished without his original bold brushstrokes.

Not only did Franz Alexander bequeath to us the very foundation stones of psychosomatic medicine, he also helped to mould many other branches of psychological science. For instance, he became one of the first practitioners to apply depth psychology to the field of criminology. Alexander authored a number of important studies which explored the unconscious roots of criminality (e.g., Alexander and Staub, 1929a, 1929b; Alexander and Healy, 1935), and, additionally, he championed the humane treatment of those who had committed serious offences. For instance, in 1959, he offered assistance to Princesse Marie Bonaparte, the French psychoanalyst who campaigned, albeit unsuccessfully, to commute the death sentence against the convicted American felon Caryl Chessman (Bertin, 1982).

Furthermore, Alexander made huge contributions to the study of psychoanalytical technique through his pioneering investigations into the value of brief psychotherapy; and he also explored the potential curative properties of the psychotherapeutic relationship itself, providing patients with a "corrective emotional experience" (Alexander, 1946, p. 66). Additionally, Alexander helped to create an empirically-based psychoanalysis, and became one of the first to undertake laboratory-style, controlled, empirical research, propelling psychoanalysis away from its longstanding reliance on the single case history towards a more broad-based study of larger sample sizes (e.g., Alexander and Wilson, 1935; cf. Alexander, 1941, 1948, 1954). As Alexander (1940, p. 314) argued with great prescience, some three-quarters of a century ago, "It will not be long before the traditional tendency of psychoanalysis for isolation and the refutation of the need for experimental validation of its findings will cede to a demand for greater conceptual clarity, for quantitative methods, the introduction of experimental procedures, and the coordination of psychoanalytic findings with physiology and the social sciences".

In his later years, Alexander also made several crucial contributions to the field of psychiatric and psychoanalytical historiography, chronicling the very origins of the mental health profession. First, he arranged for the publication of a selection of letters between Sigmund Freud and the famous Swiss psychiatrist Eugen Bleuler (Alexander and Selesnick, 1965). Thereafter, he produced two major works of historical scholarship, each quite groundbreaking in the 1960s. His posthumously-published book on *The History of Psychiatry: An Evaluation of Psychiatric Thought and Practice from Prehistoric Times to the Present*, co-authored by Sheldon Selesnick (Alexander and Selesnick, 1966), remains, in my estimation, one of the best written textbooks on psychiatric history of all time. Likewise, Alexander's book *Psychoanalytic Pioneers* (which also appeared in print after his death), co-edited by Samuel Eisenstein and Martin Grotjahn, deserves a wider audience among contemporary students, as it remains arguably the best introduction to the lives and careers of so many of the personalities who inhabited the early psychoanalytical community (Alexander, Eisenstein, and Grotjahn, 1966).

A man of great foresight, Alexander anticipated numerous important developments in the mental health field. His pioneering research in psychosomatic medicine led the way to the creation of the increasingly gargantuan specialities of health psychology and psychoneuroimmunology, exploring the impact of mental states upon bodily processes and diseases (e.g., Schlaegel and Hoyt, 1957; Sifneos, 1965; Sperling, 1978; Christie and Mellett, 1981; Fava and Wise, 1987; Taylor, 1987; Cheren, 1989a, 1989b; Blumenfield and Strain, 2006; cf. Freeman, 1973; Martin, 1997; Sternberg, 2000; Scarf, 2004; Leader and Corfield, 2007; O'Sullivan, 2015). Moreover, Alexander's attempts to understand the psychodynamics of criminality helped to provide the foundations for forensic psychotherapy and forensic psychoanalysis—offering treatment to criminals rather than punishment (e.g., Welldon, 1994, 2011; Cordess and Cox, 1996a, 1996b; Welldon and Van Velsen, 1997; Kahr, 2001; Corbett, 2014). His work on the "corrective emotional experience" and on the importance of the psychotherapeutic relationship has since become a central platform within modern relationally-orientated and attachment-orientated schools of psychoanalysis (e.g., Wachtel, 2008; cp. Willock, 2007). Even his seemingly egghead interest in the history of psychiatry and psychoanalysis contributed greatly towards the development of these areas of study as increasingly serious specialities; and thanks, in part, to Alexander's sponsorship of these particular interests, the mental health professions now enjoy at least two substantial English-language periodicals devoted exclusively to these subjects, namely, *History of Psychiatry* and, also, *Psychoanalysis and History*.

It would not be unreasonable to argue that Franz Alexander laid much of the bedrock for virtually every area of preoccupation and interest among contemporary mental health workers. In this respect, like Sigmund Freud before him, Alexander may well be the true *uomo universale* of psychoanalysis.

Alexander made not only voluminous contributions to these many aforementioned subdivisions of mental health theory and practice but, also, he distinguished himself as a writer of numerous substantial books, chapters, and essays. Additionally, he helped to shape the field of psychoanalysis by serving as the founder of the Institute for Psychoanalysis, Chicago, and as President of the American Psychoanalytic Association and, furthermore, as one of the world's very first professors of psychoanalysis at no fewer than two separate universities. And no one worked more tirelessly than Alexander to integrate psychoanalysis into mainstream American psychiatry during the 1930s, 1940s, and 1950s (e.g., Alexander, 1931, 1964). Consequently, he took great pride, one imagines, when, in 1939, he wrote to Dr. Ernest Jones, then President of the International Psycho-Analytical Association, that psychoanalysis had become nothing less than "a part of American medicine" (Alexander, 1939d; cp. Levine, 1953).

The first person to enrol in, and to graduate from, a psychoanalytical training institute, Franz Alexander earned the affection and admiration of many Continental analysts, not least of Freud himself. And before long, Alexander had developed such a trusted reputation, that he undertook the analysis of Sigmund Freud's middle son Oliver Freud (Roazen, 1975, 1993; Young-Bruehl, 1988); and, according to rumours may even have treated Freud's grandson Ernst Halberstadt as well (Roazen, n.d. [a], n.d. [b]; cf. Freud and Martin, 1985).

And yet, in spite of Alexander's unparalleled contributions—rich in depth and heft—to so many fields of psychology, he has become in many respects an increasingly forgotten figure. While his name may still be appreciated in psychoanalytical circles in Chicago, Illinois, and also in California—his one-time residences—very few young students of psychology, psychotherapy, or even psychoanalysis in other parts of the world will recognise his name. In Great Britain, he remains a shadowy figure. Certainly, I cannot remember ever hearing his name mentioned in lectures or seminars at the Tavistock Clinic, where I trained, and then worked, for many years. When Alexander's name does crop up nowadays in psychoanalytical circles, it often appears in a critical context, as for instance, in Dr. Hanna Segal's (1990) antagonistic essay about Alexander's notion of the corrective emotional experience (cp. Sandler, Kennedy, and Tyson, 1980).

Professor Leo Rangell (2004, p. 299), a former President of both the American Psychoanalytic Association and of the International

Psycho-Analytical Association, described Alexander as a neo-Freudian in the tradition of Alfred Adler and Sándor Ferenczi—in other words, a renegade—and recalled that even the other rebels, such as Dr. Heinz Kohut, actually "bristled" at the thought of being compared to Franz Alexander. In similar vein, Professor Robert Wallerstein, also a quondam President of the International Psycho-Analytical Association, referred to Alexander as one of the "heretics" of American psychoanalysis (Quoted in Di Donna, 2010, p. 635).

Consequently, as the psychoanalytical historian Professor Paul Roazen (2000, p. 20) remarked, Franz Alexander has become "unduly neglected today" and also "marginalized" (Roazen, 2000, p. 162). Several years later, Roazen (2005, p. 11) wrote about him even more frankly, arguing that, "by now Alexander's name has virtually disappeared from public memory". Roazen may perhaps have overstated his case somewhat; and Alexander enthusiasts will be delighted to know that in recent years, historians have begun to resurrect his work and his contributions in a serious manner (e.g., Makari, 2008, 2012; Möhle, 2010; Schmidt, 2010; Melcher, 2013). But I feel fairly confident that if I mentioned the name of Franz Alexander to a group of British psychoanalytical students today, most, if not all of them, would look blank or bewildered.

Alexander's works on psychosomatic medicine, in particular—once his calling card—have become the object of a great deal of harsh criticism, quite unfairly in my estimation. In his study on the history of psychosomatics, Professor Edward Shorter (1992, p. 261) spoke of Alexander's work in this field as having fallen into "disrepute"; and in a subsequent work, Shorter (1994, p. 200) referred to Alexander's research as "out of fashion today". In similar vein, Dr. Esther Sternberg (2000, p. 11), a medical researcher, also described Alexander's contributions as full of "disrepute", noting that, "the idea of blaming it all on mother seems too pat and rooted in another century" (Sternberg, 2000, p. 145). Regrettably, both Shorter and Sternberg dismissed Alexander's psychosomatic labours in too speedy a fashion; and Sternberg's characterisation of this work as based on maternal blame does not do justice to the nuance of Alexander's multi-decade labours in this field.

How and *why* did a man of such magnitude become so comparatively neglected? Why has Franz Alexander not joined the ranks of Wilfred Bion, John Bowlby, Sándor Ferenczi, Melanie Klein, Heinz Kohut, and Donald Winnicott? And why has no publisher sponsored a multi-volume edition of *The Collected Works of Franz Alexander*?

The answer to such a question might require an entire monograph on the role of orthodoxy and dissidence in the history of psychoanalysis (e.g., Bergmann, 2004; cf. Makari, 2008) and I shall not attempt to offer an explanation in this context. Fortunately, Ilonka Venier Alexander's new book, *The Life and Times of Franz Alexander: From Budapest to California*— a devoted tribute to her beloved grandfather—not only resurrects the Alexanderian legacy, reminding us of his behemoth contributions but, also, offers us a deeply tender and touching portrait that only an intimate family member could provide. To the best of my knowledge, this may well be the first full-length biography of a major psychoanalyst written by a grandchild; and as such, it has all the benefits of being both highly personalised and well-informed but also sufficiently objective and therefore protected from the dangers of idealisation or denigration.

Ilonka Alexander has researched her family history thoroughly, unearthing important new data from archives and from other genealogical repositories; and she has chosen to share some long-buried secrets, which she imparts to her readers in a deeply generous, sympathetic, and non-salacious manner. In doing so, Ms. Alexander has shed further light on the rich and multi-faceted character of her grandfather, and on his struggles against anti-Semitism, as well as on his valiant efforts to champion a rather unpopular field of endeavour, namely, psychoanalysis itself. Consequently, Ms. Alexander—a clinician in her own right— succeeds in her goal of introducing us (or reintroducing us) to Franz Alexander as a private family man and as a world leader in psychiatry and psychoanalysis, and she does so brilliantly, writing with warmth, engagement, and detail.

As a longstanding "fan" of Franz Alexander, I had already read a great deal about him, and I have had the privilege of studying his papers in various archives; nevertheless, Ms. Alexander's memoir contains *so* much new information that I found myself gripped throughout. Ms. Alexander has thus succeeded in enhancing my interest in her grandfather even more, and has stimulated a desire to re-read many of his published works.

So why has Alexander not become more "mainstream" within institutional psychoanalysis? By embracing the possibility of brief psychotherapy, he certainly angered many Freudian purists. But I suspect that Alexander also evoked an immense amount of envy during his lifetime (and perhaps even afterwards) owing to his extraordinary intelligence, his closeness to Freud, and his huge capacity for creative work. Ilonka Alexander's memoir has also helped me to appreciate that her grandfather's considerable professional and financial success may well have stimulated further primitive envy among his colleagues. After all, Franz Alexander charged extremely high professional fees (rumoured to be in excess of $100 per hour—a gargantuan sum in the mid-twentieth century), and he bestrode the psychoanalytical community in beautifully tailored suits, and employed his own chauffeur, to boot. One wonders what visceral impact Alexander must have made upon his contemporaries.

Ilonka Alexander has painted a portrait of her grandfather's success—professional, academic, economic, and so forth—and, moreover, she has helped us to understand quite a lot about the ostensibly glamorous world in which he travelled. His Chicago patients included the notorious gangster Al Capone; and during his final years in California, he treated a great many film stars, many of whom the young Ilonka recognised walking in and out of the family home for sessions with her grandfather. Franz Alexander lived next door to Frederick Loewe, the composer of the iconic Broadway musical *My Fair Lady*; and he played golf with the comedian and film star Danny Kaye. As a child, Ilonka attended school with the children of Joan Crawford and Ronald Reagan; and Ilonka's mother, Silvia, would drive her daughter to school in a Packard car—a gift from Franz Alexander—which had once belonged to Clark Gable and Carole Lombard. Thus, from Ms. Alexander's book, we obtain unique first-hand information about the way in which Franz Alexander positioned himself in the very centre of American popular culture, and in doing so may well have helped to incorporate psychoanalysis and its ideologies into the mainstream as well.

But Ilonka Venier Alexander's lovely new book, which we include with pride and delight in our History of Psychoanalysis Series, provides not only a unique portrait of one of the world's most creative and inspiring mental health professionals, it also chronicles her own very personal journey of discovery about her family's hidden Judaism. In this respect, the book constitutes not only a contribution to the history of psychoanalysis but, also, serves as a painful and lingering reminder of the centuries-long struggle against hatred and intolerance.

Alexander personified a philosophy of creativity and open-mindedness that may be quite rare among some of the more sectarian refugee psychoanalysts of his generation who strove for homogeneity rather than for difference, in the hope of creating a safe enclave for themselves. When Dr. Edward Glover, the distinguished

Scottish-born psychoanalyst resigned from membership in the British Psycho-Analytical Society in 1944, owing to complex personal and theoretical differences with his colleagues, he became something of a pariah in London; but Franz Alexander wrote to him with great sympathy, arguing that scientific disagreements should not be settled through resignation of professional affiliations and secession but, rather, through discourse, noting that, "we feel that differences of opinion in a scientific society are not only unavoidable but highly desirable" (Alexander, n.d. [c. 1949], p. 158), and that, "a homogeneous attitude about scientific matters which are still in flux" runs contrary to good science (Alexander, n.d. [c. 1949], p. 159). Such a quality of intellectual tolerance remains truly rare in the psychological disciplines, and I suspect that we might all benefit from a dose of Alexanderian thinking of this sort. Fortunately, Ms. Alexander's book about her grandfather brings him back on the map in a clear and inspiring manner.

I congratulate Ilonka Venier Alexander on her lovely biography and memoir and I recommend *The Life and Times of Franz Alexander: From Budapest to California* with deep enthusiasm. Those colleagues who already possess a great deal of knowledge about Alexander's life and professional contributions will, I have no doubt, still find many new discoveries in Ms. Alexander's book that will both please and inform. And those who have not yet encountered this remarkable man could wish for no better introduction.

Professor Brett Kahr
Series Co-Editor
History of Psychoanalysis Series
London,
June 2015

References

Alexander, Franz (1926). Neurosis and the Whole Personality. *International Journal of Psycho-Analysis, 7*, 340–352.

Alexander, Franz (1927). *Psychoanalyse der Gesamtpersönlichkeit: Neun Vorlesungen über die Anwendung von Freuds Ichtheorie auf die Neurosenlehre.* Vienna: Internationaler Psychoanalytischer Verlag.

Alexander, Franz (1931). Psychoanalysis in the Education of Psychiatrists. *American Journal of Orthopsychiatry, 1*, 362–370.

Alexander, Franz (1939a). Psychological Aspects of Medicine. *Psychosomatic Medicine, 1*, 7–18.

Alexander, Franz (1939b). Psychoanalytic Study of a Case of Essential Hypertension. *Psychosomatic Medicine, 1*, 139–152.

Alexander, Franz (1939c). Emotional Factors in Essential Hypertension: Presentation of a Tentative Hypothesis. *Psychosomatic Medicine, 1*, 173–179.

Alexander, Franz (1939d). Letter to Ernest Jones. 11th February. Folder AF4. Box AF1–4. Freud Museum, Swiss Cottage, London.

Alexander, Franz (1940). A Jury Trial of Psychoanalysis. *Journal of Abnormal and Social Psychology, 35*, 305–323.

Alexander, Franz (1941). Statistical Dream Studies on Asthma Patients. In Thomas M. French, Franz Alexander, Catherine L. Bacon, Siegfried Bernfeld, Edwin Eisler, Eugene Falstein, Margaret Gerard, Helen Vincent McLean, George J. Mohr, Ben Z. Rappaport, Helen Ross, Leon J. Saul, Lucia E. Tower, and George W. Wilson. *Psychogenic Factors in Bronchial Asthma: Part I*, pp. 62–69. Washington, D.C.: National Research Council.

Alexander, Franz (1946). The Principle of Corrective Emotional Experience. In Franz Alexander, Thomas Morton French, Catherine Lillie Bacon, Therese Benedek, Rudolf A. Fuerst, Margaret Wilson Gerard, Roy Richard Grinker, Martin Grotjahn, Adelaide McFadyen Johnson, Helen Vincent McLean, and Edoardo Weiss. *Psychoanalytic Therapy: Principles and Application*, pp. 66–70. New York: Ronald Press Company.

Alexander, Franz (1948). The Role of the Scientist in Society—I. In Lawson G. Lowrey and Victoria Sloane (Eds.). *Orthopsychiatry: 1923–1948. Retrospect and Prospect*, pp. 342–358. n.p.: American Orthopsychiatric Association.

Alexander, Franz (1954). Some Quantitative Aspects of Psychoanalytic Technique. *Journal of the American Psychoanalytic Association, 2*, 685–701.

Alexander, Franz (1957). Psychosomatische Wechselbeziehungen. In Alexander Mitscherlich (Ed.). *Freud in der Gegenwart: Ein Vortragszyklus der Universitäten Frankfurt und Heidelberg zum hundertsten Geburtstag*, pp. 279–306. Frankfurt am Main: Europäische Verlagsanstalt.

Alexander, Franz (1960). *The Western Mind in Transition: An Eyewitness Story.* New York: Random House.

Alexander, Franz (1964). Current Problems in Psychosomatic Medicine: (Abstract). *Psychosomatics, 5*, 1–3.

Alexander, Franz (n.d. [c. 1949]). Letter to Edward Glover. n.d. Quoted in Edward Glover (1949). Letter to LeRoy Maeder. 3rd July. In Paul Roazen (2000). *Oedipus in Britain: Edward Glover and the Struggle Over Klein*, pp. 158–161. New York: Other/Other Press.

Alexander, Franz; French, Thomas M., and Pollock, George H. (Eds.). (1968). *Psychosomatic Specificity: Volume 1. Experimental Study and Results.* Chicago, Illinois: University of Chicago Press.

Alexander, Franz; Eisenstein, Samuel, and Grotjahn, Martin (Eds.). (1966). *Psychoanalytic Pioneers.* New York: Basic Books.

Alexander, Franz, and Healy, William (1935). *Roots of Crime: Psychoanalytic Studies.* New York: Alfred A. Knopf.

Alexander, Franz, and Selesnick, Sheldon T. (1965). Freud-Bleuler Correspondence. *Archives of General Psychiatry, 12*, 1–9.

Alexander, Franz G., and Selesnick, Sheldon T. (1966). *The History of Psychiatry: An Evaluation of Psychiatric Thought and Practice from Prehistoric Times to the Present.* New York: Harper and Row, Publishers.

Alexander, Franz, and Staub, Hugo (1929a). *Der Verbrecher und seine Richter: Ein psychoanalytischer Einblick in die Welt der Paragraphen.* Vienna: Internationaler Psychoanalytischer Verlag.

Alexander, Franz, and Staub, Hugo (1929b). Der Kampf ums Recht. *Die Psychoanalytische Bewegung, 1*, 117–122.

Alexander, Franz, and Szasz, Thomas S. (1952). The Psychosomatic Approach in Medicine. In Franz Alexander and Helen Ross (Eds.). *Dynamic Psychiatry*, pp. 369–400. Chicago, Illinois: University of Chicago Press.

Alexander, Franz, and Wilson, George W. (1935). Quantitative Dream Studies: A Methodological Attempt at a Quantitative Evaluation of Psychoanalytic Material. *Psychoanalytic Quarterly, 4*, 371–407.

Bergmann, Martin S. (2004). Rethinking Dissidence and Change in the History of Psychoanalysis. In Martin S. Bergmann (Ed.). *Understanding Dissidence and Controversy in the History of Psychoanalysis*, pp. 1–109. New York: Other/Other Press.

Bertin, Célia (1982). *La Dernière Bonaparte.* Paris: Librairie Académique Perrin.

Blumenfield, Michael, and Strain, James J. (Eds.). (2006). *Psychosomatic Medicine.* Philadelphia, Pennsylvania: Lippincott Williams and Wilkins/ Wolters Kluwer Business.

Brown, Theodore M. (1987). Alan Gregg and the Rockefeller Foundation's Support of Franz Alexander's Psychosomatic Research. *Bulletin of the History of Medicine, 61*, 155–182.

Cheren, Stanley (Ed.). (1989a). *Psychosomatic Medicine: Theory, Physiology, and Practice. Volume I.* Madison, Connecticut: International Universities Press.

Cheren, Stanley (Ed.). (1989b). *Psychosomatic Medicine: Theory, Physiology, and Practice. Volume II.* Madison, Connecticut: International Universities Press.

Christie, Margaret J., and Mellett, Peter G. (Eds.). (1981). *Foundations of Psychosomatics.* Chichester, West Sussex: John Wiley and Sons.

Corbett, Alan (2014). *Disabling Perversions: Forensic Psychotherapy with People with Intellectual Disabilities*. London: Karnac Books.

Cordess, Christopher, and Cox, Murray (Eds.). (1996a). *Forensic Psychotherapy: Crime, Psychodynamics and the Offender Patient. Volume I. Mainly Theory*. London: Jessica Kingsley Publishers.

Cordess, Christopher, and Cox, Murray (Eds.). (1996b). *Forensic Psychotherapy: Crime, Psychodynamics and the Offender Patient. Volume II. Mainly Practice*. London: Jessica Kingsley Publishers.

Deutsch, Felix (Ed.). (1953). *The Psychosomatic Concept in Psychoanalysis*. New York: International Universities Press.

Deutsch, Felix (Ed.). (1959). *On the Mysterious Leap from the Mind to the Body: A Workshop Study on the Theory of Conversion*. New York: International Universities Press.

Deutsch, Felix, and Kauf, Emil (1924). *Herz und Sport: Klinische Untersuchungen über die Einwirkung des Sportes auf das Herz*. Berlin: Urban und Schwarzenberg.

Deutsch, Felix; Thompson, Donald; Pinderhughes, Charles, and Goodglass, Harold (1962a). Body, Mind, and the Sensory Gateways. *Fortschritte der Psychosomatischen Medizin, 2*, 1–106.

Deutsch, Felix; Thompson, Donald; Pinderhughes, Charles, and Goodglass, Harold (1962b). *Body, Mind and the Sensory Gateways*. New York: Basic Books.

Di Donna, Luca (2010). The Life and Work of Robert S. Wallerstein: A Conversation. *American Imago, 67*, 617–658.

Dunbar, H. Flanders (1935). *Emotions and Bodily Changes: A Survey of Literature on Psychosomatic Interrelationships. 1910–1933*. New York: Columbia Univeristy Press.

Dunbar, Flanders (1943). *Psychosomatic Diagnosis*. New York: Paul B. Hoeber/Medical Book Department of Harper and Brothers.

Dunbar, Flanders (1947). *Mind and Body: Psychosomatic Medicine*. New York: Random House.

Dunbar, Flanders (1959). *Psychiatry in the Medical Specialties*. New York: Blakiston Division, McGraw-Hill Book Company/Landsberger Medical Books.

Dunbar, Flanders; Arlow, Jacob; Hussey, Raymond; Lewin, Bertram; Lowe, Robert C., Rubin, Sydney; Schneider, E., and Sontag, Lester W. (1948). *Synopsis of Psychosomatic Diagnosis and Treatment*. St. Louis, Missouri: C. V. Mosby Company.

Fava, Giovanni A., and Wise, Thomas N. (Eds.). (1987). *Research Paradigms in Psychosomatic Medicine*. Basel: Karger/S. Karger.

Freeman, Lucy (1956). *Hospital in Action: The Story of the Michael Reese Medical Center*. New York: Rand McNally and Company.

Freeman, Lucy (1973). *Your Mind Can Stop the Common Cold*. New York: Peter H. Wyden.

Freud, W. Ernest, and Martin, Jay (1985). A Conversation. *Psychoanalytic Education, 4*, 29–56.

Fuechtner, Veronika (2011). *Berlin Psychoanalytic: Psychoanalysis and Culture in Weimar Republic Germany and Beyond*. Berkeley, California: University of California Press.

Grinker, Roy R. (1953). *Psychosomatic Research*. New York: W. W. Norton and Company.

Grinker, Roy R., and Spiegel, John P. (1943). *War Neuroses in North Africa: The Tunisian Campaign. (January-May 1943)*. New York: Josiah Macy, Jr. Foundation.

Grinker, Roy R., and Spiegel, John P. (1945). *War Neuroses*. Philadelphia, Pennsylvania: Blakiston/Blakiston Company.

Ham, George C., Alexander, Franz, and Carmichael, Hugh T. (1950). Dynamic Aspects of the Personality Features and Reactions Characteristic of Patients with Graves Disease. In Harold G. Wolff, Stewart G. Wolf, Jr., and Clarence C. Hare (Eds.). *Life Stress and Bodily Disease: Proceedings of the Association. December 2 and 3, 1949. New York, N.Y.*, pp. 451–457. Baltimore, Maryland: Williams and Wilkins Company.

Harrington, Anne (2008). *The Cure Within: A History of Mind-Body Medicine*. New York: W. W. Norton and Company.

Kahr, Brett (Ed.). (2001). *Forensic Psychotherapy and Psychopathology: Winnicottian Perspectives*. London: H. Karnac (Books).

Kardiner, Abram (1932). *The Bio-Analysis of the Epileptic Reaction*. Albany, New York: Psychoanalytic Quarterly Press.

Kardiner, Abram (1941). *The Traumatic Neuroses of War*. Washington, D.C.: National Research Council.

Kardiner, Abram, and Spiegel, Herbert (1947). *War Stress and Neurotic Illness*. New York: Paul B. Hoeber/Medical Book Department of Harper and Brothers.

Leader, Darian, and Corfield, David (2007). *Why Do People Get Ill?* London: Hamish Hamilton/Penguin Books.

Levine, Maurice (1953). The Impact of Psychoanalysis on Training in Psychiatry. In Franz Alexander and Helen Ross (Eds.). *20 Years of Psychoanalysis: A Symposium in Celebration of the Twentieth Anniversary of the Chicago Institute for Psychoanalysis*, pp. 50–66. New York: W. W. Norton and Company.

Lipsitt, Don R. (2000). Psyche and Soma: Struggles to Close the Gap. In Roy W. Menninger and John C. Nemiah (Eds.). *American Psychiatry After World War II: (1944–1994)*, pp. 152–186. Washington, D.C.: American Psychiatric Press.

Lipsitt, Don R. (2006). Psychosomatic Medicine: History of a "New" Specialty. In Michael Blumenfield and James J. Strain (Eds.). (2006). *Psychosomatic Medicine*, pp. 3–20. Philadelphia, Pennsylvania: Lippincott Williams and Wilkins/Wolters Kluwer Business.

Makari, George (2008). *Revolution in Mind: The Creation of Psychoanalysis*. New York: Harper/HarperCollins Publishers.

Makari, George (2012). *Mitteleuropa on the Hudson: On the Struggle for American Psychoanalysis After the Anschluß*. In John C. Burnham (Ed.). *After Freud Left: A Century of Psychoanalysis in America*, pp. 111–124. Chicago, Illinois: University of Chicago Press.

Martin, Paul (1997). *The Sickening Mind: Brain, Behaviour, Immunity and Disease*. Hammersmith, London: HarperCollins Publishers.

Melcher, Imke (2013). *Franz Alexander und die moderne Psychotherapie*. Gießen: Psychosozial-Verlag.

Möhle, Sebastian (2010). *Die erste Generation der deutschen Psychosomatik: Frühe psychoanalytische Ansätze und Entwicklungen*. Hamburg: Verlag Dr. Kovač.

O'Sullivan, Suzanne (2015). *It's All in Your Head: True Stories of Imaginary Illness*. London: Chatto and Windus/Vintage/Penguin Random House, Penguin Random House UK.

Rangell, Leo (2004). *My Life in Theory*. Fred Busch (Ed.). New York: Other/Other Press.

Roazen, Paul (n.d. [a]). Interview with Martin Grotjahn. n.d. Cited in Paul Roazen (1975). *Freud and His Followers*. New York: Alfred A. Knopf.

Roazen, Paul (n.d. [b]). Interview with Robert Jokl. n.d. Cited in Paul Roazen (1975). *Freud and His Followers*. New York: Alfred A. Knopf.

Roazen, Paul (1993). *Meeting Freud's Family*. Amherst, Massachusetts: University of Massachusetts Press.

Roazen, Paul (2000). *Oedipus in Britain: Edward Glover and the Struggle Over Klein*. New York: Other/Other Press.

Roazen, Paul (2005). *Edoardo Weiss: The House That Freud Built*. New Brunswick, New Jersey: Transaction Publishers.

Sandler, Joseph; Kennedy, Hansi, and Tyson, Robert L. (1980). *The Technique of Child Psychoanalysis: Discussions with Anna Freud*. Cambridge, Massachusetts: Harvard University Press.

Scarf, Maggie (2004). *Secrets, Lies, Betrayals: How the Body Holds the Secrets of Life and How to Unlock Them*. New York: Random House.

Schaegel, Theodore F., Jr., and Hoyt, Millard (1957). *Psychosomatic Ophthalmology*. Baltimore, Maryland: Williams and Wilkins Company.

Schmidt, Erika S. (2010). The Berlin Tradition in Chicago: Franz Alexander and the Chicago Institute for Psychoanalysis. *Psychoanalysis and History*, 12, 69–83.

Segal, Hanna (1990). Some Comments on the Alexander Technique. *Psychoanalytic Inquiry*, *10*, 409–414.

Shorter, Edward (1992). *From Paralysis to Fatigue: A History of Psycho-somatic Illness in the Modern Era*. New York: Free Press/Macmillan/Maxwell Macmillan International/Maxwell Communication Group of Companies.

Shorter, Edward (1994). *From the Mind into the Body: The Cultural Origins of Psychosomatic Symptoms*. New York: Free Press/Macmillan/Maxwell Macmillan International/Maxwell Communication Group of Companies.

Sifneos, Peter E. (1965). *Ascent from Chaos: A Psychosomatic Case Study*. Cambridge, Massachusetts: Harvard University Press, and London: Oxford University Press.

Sperling, Melitta (1978). *Psychosomatic Disorders in Childhood*. Otto E. Sperling (Ed.). New York: Jason Aronson.

Sternberg, Esther M. (2000). *The Balance Within: The Science Connecting Health and Emotions*. New York: W.H. Freeman and Company.

Taylor, Graeme J. (1987). *Psychosomatic Medicine and Contemporary Psycho-analysis*. Madison, Connecticut: International Universities Press.

Wachtel, Paul L. (2008). *Relational Theory and the Practice of Psychotherapy*. New York: Guilford Press/Guilford Publications.

Weiner, Herbert (2008). Psychosomatic Medicine and the Mind-Body Relation: Historical, Philosophical, Scientific, and Clinical Perspec-tives. In Edwin R. Wallace IV and John Gach (Eds.). *History of Psychiatry and Medical Psychology: With an Epilogue on Psychiatry and the Mind-Body Relation*, pp. 781–834. New York: Springer/Springer-Science and Business Media.

Welldon, Estela V. (1994). Forensic Psychotherapy. In Petruska Clarkson and Michael Pokorny (Eds.). *The Handbook of Psychotherapy*, pp. 470–493. London: Routledge.

Welldon, Estela V. (2011). *Playing with Dynamite: A Personal Approach to the Psychoanalytic Understanding of Perversions, Violence, and Criminality*. London: Karnac Books.

Welldon, Estela V., and Van Velsen, Cleo (Eds.). (1997). *A Practical Guide to Forensic Psychotherapy*. London: Jessica Kingsley Publishers.

Will, Herbert (1984). *Die Geburt der Psychosomatik: Georg Groddeck—der Mensch und Wissenschaftler*. Munich: Urban und Schwarzenberg.

Willock, Brent (2007). *Comparative-Integrative Psychoanalysis: A Relational Perspective for the Discipline's Second Century*. New York: Analytic Press/Taylor and Francis Group.

Young-Bruehl, Elisabeth (1988). *Anna Freud: A Biography*. New York: Summit Books/Simon and Schuster.

PREFACE

I often thought of writing a biography of my grandfather that would also include memories of my life with him. In fact, many years ago, a former employer and friend, Dr. Jane Matson, a school psychologist, suggested that I write a book about my family. A family that had at its core a very important man, Dr. Franz Alexander, the founder of the Chicago Institute for Psychoanalysis and the man, who, it turns out, shaped my life from the time I was a newborn. It was not until I retired from a successful thirty-year career as a clinical social worker, and began to research the genealogical history of the family, that I decided the timing was right to tell his story. As I review my experiences and memories with my grandparents, I realize that my story, and the story of the influence my grandfather had on my life, is not normal. Growing up I did not truly understand my experience was so unusual. It was all I knew at the time.

I did not know of Franz Alexander's importance to the world until my mother helped me to understand. She once told me about his obtaining grants from the Rockefeller Foundation. I thought she meant that the Rockefellers had invited him to come to America. This sounded special and impressive to me as a young child. It was only in adulthood that I came to understand what she meant. "Your grandfather is as important to psychoanalysis as Elvis is to music." She said this to me one Christmas, driving home from time spent in the Palm Springs house. Now that was something I could understand. Again, I was impressed. He was to me just my grandfather, my Big Papa, who played the role of father too. He bought me expensive gifts, was happy to spend time with me, and was jolly. I remembered writing letters to him from private school, when he was still in Chicago and putting the initials "MD" after his name which was preceded by "Dr." It had no meaning to me. I was seven years old.

I recall another time. I was in my grandfather's office in 1957 or 1958, waiting for him to finish with patients so we could go out together to eat dinner. He so disliked eating alone. As I looked around the office my eyes stopped on a portrait painted by my grandmother. It was a very large painting of Professor Freud looking very distinguished and important. I asked my mother who was in the painting. I had not seen it before as it was previously in the Chicago office, where I had never been. My grandfather overheard my question. He was astonished and surprised, nearly flabbergasted, that I did not know who Freud was, even at the age of twelve or thirteen. My mother said, "Papa, she is just a little girl. Of course she does not know about Freud." I guess he could not imagine that his granddaughter would not know this very important man.

Well, more than fifty years later, as a psychotherapist myself, I certainly know who Freud is, the impact and importance he had on the world, the impact and importance he had on my grandfather, and on my own career as well. I, too, know of the impact my grandfather had on the world and the field of psychoanalysis, psychotherapy, and psychosomatic medicine. Many of his ideas were ahead of the times in which he lived, though he was criticized by many and his work in 1946 precipitated, some say, a crisis in the field. Ironically and interestingly, there is renewed interest today in his work and many of his ideas and concepts are practised today without consideration for their controversial beginnings.

In recent years I have learned of the even bigger impact he had on my life. As I uncover more of his life, and the decisions he made affecting us all, and the ways in which he kept certain topics and truths under wraps, he continues to impact my life. In the spring of 2010 I began to know my new-found family and to learn of those who came before me. It is my belief that you cannot know yourself until you know your own personal history and from where you came. Since that time it has been a journey of discovery with many extraordinary stories and people along the way. It is the interweaving of my own discovery of my grandfather's family that has led me to write an intimate biography of Franz Alexander. It is in these last few years that I have really come to know him.

This biography of my grandfather, Dr. Franz Alexander, describes his family, the time in which he grew up and studied, and the decisions and challenges he faced emigrating from Europe to America, and his founding of the Chicago Institute for Psychoanalysis. It is his personal and private story, intertwined with the new discovery of family. It is also the story of half-truths, hidden information, betrayal, confusion, fear, and sadness across the last 150 years that turns itself into a story of hope, love of family, new chances and, finally, a happy ending. It is written with respect and awe for his accomplishments as well as love and appreciation for the gifts he gave me as his granddaughter.

As Martin Grotjahn wrote in *Psychoanalytic Pioneers* in 1966, in the book coedited by my grandfather, "To write a profile of Franz Alexander is to present a panoramic view of psychoanalytic development in Europe and in the United States of America."

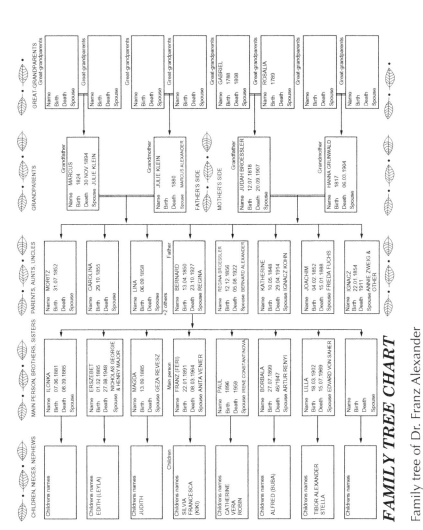

FAMILY TREE CHART

Family tree of Dr. Franz Alexander

GREAT-GRANDPARENTS
Great-grandparents

Great-grandparents
Name	MARCUS
Birth	1824
Death	30 NOV 1894
Spouse	JULIE KLEIN

Great-grandparents
Name	
Birth	
Death	
Spouse	

Great-grandparents
Name	
Birth	
Death	
Spouse	

Great-grandparents
Name	GABRIEL
Birth	1788
Death	1808
Spouse	

Great-grandparents
Name	ROSALIA
Birth	1789
Death	
Spouse	

Great-grandparents
Name	
Birth	
Death	
Spouse	

Great-grandparents
Name	
Birth	
Death	
Spouse	

GRANDPARENTS

Grandfather
Name	MARCUS
Birth	1824
Death	30 NOV 1894
Spouse	JULIE KLEIN

Grandmother
Name	JULIE KLEIN
Birth	1880
Death	
Spouse	MARCUS ALEXANDER

FATHER'S SIDE

MOTHER'S SIDE

Grandfather
Name	JUDAH BROESSLER
Birth	12.07.1818
Death	20.09.1907
Spouse	

Grandmother
Name	HANNA GRUNWALD
Birth	1817
Death	06.03.1904
Spouse	

PARENTS, AUNTS, UNCLES

Name	MORITZ
Birth	31.07.1852
Death	
Spouse	

Name	CAROLINA
Birth	29.10.1855
Death	
Spouse	

Name	LINA
Birth	06.09.1858
Death	
Spouse	
+2 others

Father
Name	BERNARD
Birth	13.04.1850
Death	23.10.1927
Spouse	REGINA

Name	REGINA BROESSLER
Birth	12.12.1856
Death	
Spouse	BERNARD ALEXANDER

Name	KATHERINE
Birth	10.05.1848
Death	29.04.1914
Spouse	IGNACZ KOHN

Name	JOACHIM
Birth	04.02.1852
Death	15.01.1888
Spouse	FRIEDA FUCHS

Name	IGNACZ
Birth	22.01.1854
Death	1911
Spouse	ANNIE ZWEIG & OTHER

MAIN PERSON, BROTHERS, SISTERS

Name	ILONKA
Birth	07.06.1881
Death	08.09.1885
Spouse	

Name	ERSZEBET
Birth	01.02.1885
Death	27.08.1948
Spouse	NICHOLAS GEORGIE & HENRY MAJOR

Name	MAGDA
Birth	13.09.1885
Death	
Spouse	GEZA REVESZ

Main person
Name	FRANZ (FERI)
Birth	22.01.1891
Death	08.03.1964
Spouse	ANITA VENIER

Name	PAUL
Birth	1896
Death	1959
Spouse	IRENE CONSTANTINOVA

Name	BORBALA
Birth	27.07.1899
Death	46/1947
Spouse	ARTUR RENYI

Name	LILLA
Birth	18.03.1902
Death	15.07.1969
Spouse	EDVARD VON SAHER

Name	
Birth	
Death	
Spouse	

CHILDREN, NIECES, NEPHEWS

Childrens names

Childrens names
EDITH (LEYLA)

Childrens names
JUDITH

Children

Childrens names
SILVIA
FRANCESCA (KIKI)

Childrens names
CATHERINE
VERA
ROBIN

Childrens names
ALFRED (BUBA)

Childrens names
TIBOR ALEXANDER
STELLA

Childrens names

CHAPTER ONE

A journey to the past

Dr. Franz Alexander

1

I have been searching for family my entire life, never really understanding why. My father walked away from me to appease my grandfather, Dr. Franz Alexander, and my mother and I were strangers. My only family was an influential grandfather who visited from time to time and bestowed expensive gifts on me. The gifts did not help much, though, and I felt disconnected and adrift. When I decided to find out about my family, information uncovered meant I soon must grapple with the fact I might be Jewish. That is when I sought to learn more about the family. I found a cousin in Italy and another in Cleveland, Ohio: ladies whom I had never heard of before. My cousin Eva, in Cleveland, said during our first conversation, "We have been looking for you *your* whole life." When I met Eva in February of 2010, the first thing she said to me was "You are family, I love you." It was more confusing because she knew who I was. Why not vice versa? When I began to correspond with my cousin Stella she said she knew nothing of me and that my mother's whereabouts were a mystery to her father. This was untrue as my grandfather enrolled me in a boarding school and paid the tuition. He most certainly knew where she and I both were. Finally, my cousin Vera told me she frequently had Thanksgiving dinner with my grandparents while she was in college and there was never a mention of me. Absolutely nothing was shared or discussed.

I travelled to meet these ladies and began to put the pieces together. I met another cousin in Alaska and her brother and sister in Madison, Wisconsin. During my visit with Eva in Cleveland, she asked me if I knew I was Jewish. I said "No." I gradually began to meet and know of more cousins, from Australia to Austria. I began to think I was not alone. And I began to think I might just be Jewish after all. Some cousins accepted our Jewish heritage, some did not.

During the same initial trip, I met with a former director of the Chicago Institute for Psychoanalysis, Dr. David Terman, who said to me, "Everybody in Chicago knew he [my grandfather] was Jewish, but nobody talked about it." He was shocked to hear I had just, a year before, learned of my own Jewish heritage. When we discussed it, he sat straight up in his chair, as if surprised by my comments. I thought, if they all knew, why didn't I? Why didn't my mother? Why it was kept so tightly under wraps in my family is a secret too.

Eva and I hatched a plan to bring our disjointed family together. In July 2011, more than twenty-five cousins travelled from far and near to meet in La Jolla, my childhood home in California. We made my friend Julia, who was instrumental in my search for family, an honorary family member.

"When did you find out you were Jewish?" Everyone wanted to know this information from one another. Most felt alone and assumed they had no family. The secret kept from me was kept from them too, but the secret was kept from me the longest. Learning of my Jewish connection and the chance to meet previously unknown cousins was a turning point in my life. Finding family may, in the end, be the greatest gift my grandfather unknowingly gave me.

It is through this loving lens that this biography of Franz Alexander is written. He is the man who greatly influenced the world of psychoanalysis in its early days and who was the center of my world. He is still the most important person in my life.

I called him Big Papa. My grandmother and everyone in the family called him Feri, which is a shortening of his Hungarian name, Ferenc, and his closest colleagues and dearest friends called him Alex. I guess a man as large and important to the world needed many names. He was the Elvis of the psychoanalytic world in America. That is how my mother explained it to me as a child.

He was the first graduate of the Berlin Psychoanalytic Institute, although it is true there was no formal training program at the time; the man who turned down Freud's offer to enter a private practice in Vienna, and the man Freud told to go to America and spread the doctrine of psychoanalysis. Freud was fearful that America would dilute his ideas and ruin him, but he wished him well anyway. He was my grandfather, my surrogate father, and the most important person in my life. He named me after his older sister and himself. Now, more than fifty years after his death, he continues to influence me and I continue to miss him. How I wish I was older than a teen when he died in 1964.

It was during my very early years that I began to know Big Papa. I considered myself a lucky little girl to be his granddaughter. When I spent time with him I felt as though I, conversely, was the most important person in his life. That is the gift he gave to me. I know now that special connection we shared was because he had such a loving and kind childhood. He was able to give to me what he himself had received. I loved to spend time with him as he regaled me with stories. He was fun. I never thought of him as anything other than youthful.

As I have learned more about him, through family records and interviews with newly found cousins who had been kept from me, I am more impressed by his stature, compassion, contributions to the field of psychoanalysis, and his intellect yet, paradoxically, for the first time, I see him as not so perfect. Like everyone, he also had faults and limitations. His story, and my discovery of family these past few years, is intertwined. It is an unearthing of stories and people and a never-ending commitment to family. That is part of his legacy.

There is renewed interest in my grandfather's theories, and many of his ideas, considered to have been a betrayal of traditional psychoanalytic doctrine at the time, are now the norm of the American and international psychoanalytic communities. Dr. David Terman, former director of the Chicago Psychoanalytic Institute, recently said during a phone conversation to me that few in Chicago knew of my grandfather's family and he rarely spoke about personal issues. Dr. Terman suggested that to know more about my grandfather's background would help to better understand his work in the fields of psychoanalysis and psychosomatic medicine.

So, come with me to learn of the life of these fascinating Alexanders and, in particular, Franz Alexander. The journey begins in Budapest during the last days of the nineteenth century, travels to other bustling capitals in Europe, and settles in Chicago for a long time as my grandfather founds and leads the Chicago Institute for Psychoanalysis through its golden years. His journey ends with yet another move, this time to California, pushing further west, as he had even more new ideas and dreams to fulfil. The journey is not without challenges, surprises, disappointments, and triumphs. In many ways, it is like our own life's entire journey, but this one is unique to him.

Few knew him, really knew him. This is his personal and public story.

CHAPTER TWO

Life at the Palace

Budapest. For many the mere mention of the name of this beautiful city brings to mind what geography brought to it: a city cut in half by the great river Danube, the second longest in Europe. This river runs through and by some of the most lovely cities in Europe.

Budapest is steeped in history and today is modern and diverse. Many sights are the same as they appeared in the early 1900s. The Buda hills, their flowers, trees and shrubs, and open spaces grace the shores of the river just as they did in the past. The best way to arrive in Budapest was always by boat; whether you come to Budapest from Vienna or from Belgrade, the first sights are both magical and magnificent. The river bank and the ramparts lie at your feet. The view of the Chain and Elizabeth bridges, as they span the mighty Danube, and of the Parliament buildings, is breathtaking. As you take in the scene it is as if the river was invented just for the purpose of beautifying the city. Of course, it was not, but the feeling one gets, standing and experiencing the beauty, as it slowly unfolds before you, makes one wonder. It is, indeed, magical. If you are lucky to see Budapest at night, with the lights of Parliament shining on the water, you will never forget the images.

The Austro-Hungarian Compromise of 1867 recognized the two monarchies of Austria and Hungary which came to be known as the Austro-Hungarian Empire and was ruled by the Habsburgs. Subsequently, the twin cities of Buda and Pest underwent rapid growth and expansion, and finally formally merged in 1873, along with old Buda, to form Hungary's capital city, Budapest. Pest was extensively rebuilt based on the model of Paris, created by Baron Haussmann, under the direction of the Emperor Napoleon. The city continued its growth, in concentric circles like other large European cities, along existing rail lines. The main thoroughfares of Nagykörút (Great Boulevard) and the Andrassy Boulevard lead to Heroes' Square where tall marble colonnades feature statues of Hungarian heroes and politicians and the grand central column is topped with the Archangel Gabriel. (The site at night, with spotlights on the statues, takes the breath away.) The Hungarian millennium celebrations of 1896 began in Heroes' Square and an adjacent great park and its fountains, gardens, and lakes. The gardens surrounding Vajdahunyad Castle, recreated after the original castle in Transylvania, are perhaps the most extravagant example of artistry in Hungary seen at the time. They are a perfect example of the monumental scale and style that influenced the period. The square and the resplendent residences that ring the square reflect a bygone era when grace and manners were considered essential or important traits in order to live and advance in a proper society.

During this time of cultural expansion and economic development, new suburbs were created to make room for and house the rapidly growing and financially successful population. The newly emerging middle class was predominantly Magyar, although German as well as Jewish communities developed because of the large influx of immigrants flocking to the city. Although Budapest surpassed Berlin as the fastest-growing European city, the rest of Hungary continued to be rural and its people understood and accepted the old feudal ways. This class structure was complicated as the oldest, established group of aristocrats was land owners, and the newer aristocrats consisted of the financial wizards who had come into existence when Budapest's commerce grew and thrived.

The old ways of the landowner Magyar nobility were threatened as capitalism began to spread throughout Hungary, but this change was mostly witnessed in the capital city. Despite the gradual loss of land, the Magyars clung to their way of life and their customs throughout the nineteenth century. Their children were largely educated at home and then attended Catholic gymnasiums or convent schools. Most families were Catholic and some had their own priest and a private chapel. These children were cosmopolitan and studied languages, and were provided with lessons in riding and shooting, as well as the arts. It was assumed that all the lessons and study would prepare them to enter and assume their rightful place in Budapest's established society.

Beneath this so-called aristocracy was a gentry-class comprised primarily of those who owned land. This group was largely considered to be superior to those of the financial gentry, and this belief was fostered in the Alexander family as well. Many in this class left their country houses to move into the city of Budapest yet never did relinquish their property. (The Alexanders did this too, holding on to the farm and land on the outskirts of Budapest.) Many would hang on to dilapidated houses and continue to feel their sense of importance or entitlement. They were not ready to assume the role of shopkeeper, retailer, or capitalist. They would enter the government as civil servants and continue to be critical of others, especially those who were to become financially successful, the Jews. This period, between 1870 and 1900, was a time of prosperity for the Jewish community of Budapest. The community grew and played a major role in the development of the capital and the industrial boom in the region. The Habsburgs recognized their achievements and 350 Jewish families were given noble titles.

Budapest, in the early days and years of the twentieth century, and before the devastation of World War I, was a spectacular place to live and raise a family. The energy of the city and its culture rivalled Vienna and its active café society was as important as that of Paris. It was the cultural center of Eastern Europe and the city sparkled with energy and excitement as the night lights of Budapest sparkle today. Present-day Budapest, unfortunately, is no longer the center for the arts in Eastern Europe or a very happy place for Hungarians. The arts flourish no more in the capital. In fact, many say that there is a thin surface of a cultural life and wealth for foreigners only: A veneer covers up much poverty and an everyday rush to survive. Recent newspaper articles suggest at least one third of Hungarians are living in a state of poverty and another third are poor (*Budapest Beacon*, August 2014). This, in the aftermath of communism, is a negative consequence as Hungary, and other eastern European countries, struggle to find their center: some after revolution and years of instability, and some not.

The difference between the two sides of the river in 1900 was more apparent than today. The city, then as now, was divided into eleven diverse districts. The Pest side of the city is flat and industrial compared to the beauty of Buda's hills and surrounding open green spaces, glamorous spas, exclusive hotels, and majestic residential neighborhoods. The area around Castle Hill, known as District One, was the most fashionable address in Budapest at the turn of the century. The oldest residents of Budapest lived here. These wealthy and conservative families did not necessarily describe themselves as Hungarian. Many still spoke German and some of the street names reflected the area's German heritage and influence. Some street names, previously in German, were changed to Magyar around the time of the Compromise.

On the other side of the river is Pest, younger than Buda and not nearly as beautiful. In fact, the inner portion of District Four dates back to before 1800. Pest was, however, the commercial hub of the capital and what made it run. In 1900 nearly ninety percent of the people lived in Pest. Many of the finer hotels were here, near the Parliament and along the Blue Danube.

It was, however, into this prosperous, hopeful yet complicated time, just before, during, and after the celebrations of the millennium and before World War I, that the author's grandfather, Franz Alexander (Ferenc Gabor Alexander), and his siblings were born.

The family lived in District Seven, known as Erzsebetvaros (Elizabeth Town or the Elizabeth Ring), on the Pest side of the Danube. This area was named after the wife of Franz-Josef I in the late 1880s. The area near the Elizabeth Ring, in central Pest though not far from the river, was nicknamed by the literati Saint Sulpice of Budapest because it contained many extravagant residential palaces owned by Catholic aristocrats. It also contained a Catholic seminary. The Elizabeth Ring bordered the Museum District and many booksellers and retail shops lined the avenues. Erzsebetvaros also included the local synagogue, the largest in Hungary, located on Dohany Street. This synagogue is most likely to have been where the Alexanders would have worshiped had they not been baptised and raised as Roman Catholics. The family did not practise any of the Jewish rites. None of the Alexander children or grandchildren were raised Jewish. Although some learned of the family's Jewish heritage in their adult years, none accepted it as his and her own faith.

New residential areas, created during those times, are now part of today's midtown suburbs. The neighborhoods included grand houses and large apartment complexes, some with cafés and shops, and some housed municipal buildings and offices as well. This area of the city's expansion surpassed Buda and its surrounding hills and became a center for trade and commerce. The new large Jewish community played a major role in its development and expansion. Buda, old Buda, and Pest, prior to being joined, each had its own unique Jewish history and culture. The thread of a Jewish heritage and its influence will weave its way throughout the Alexander family as the years pass and the story unfolds.

Bernard Alexander began his university training close to home, in Pest, but spent only one year there. He and Regina Broessler may have met while Bernard was pursuing his university courses in Vienna. Bernard had moved there to study with Professor Robert Zimmermann who would become his mentor. Bernard devoted himself to the natural sciences, anatomy, and physiology, all of which constitute the theoretical foundation for the field of medicine. His parents, Marcus Alexander and Julie Klein, would have preferred he study medicine, but he showed no interest in medicine. Despite applying himself to what could have been considered premed or medicine, he continued to read philosophy in his spare time. While in Vienna, he also studied German and literature and he graduated with distinction when he passed his exams. He then applied for a Hungarian governmental grant to travel and further his studies abroad. He was successful and with financial backing was able to go to Germany. He travelled with his best friend, Joseph Banoczi, another Hungarian scholar who also pursued his education in Germany. Bernard studied in Gottingen, Leipzig, and Berlin, and his subjects included physiological optics with world renowned Professor Hermann von Helmholtz as well as philosophy and mathematics. Bernard eventually obtained his doctorate from the University of Leipzig in 1874. He presented his dissertation on a defence of Kant's *Critique of Pure Reason*.

Regina, the niece of a physician, was living with her family in Vienna. She was born in Ungarish Brod (now called Uhersky Brod), then part of Czechoslovakia though at the time it was part of the vast Austro-Hungarian Empire, namely Moravia. She was the fourth of five children and from a close-knit family. Bernard was the first of six children born to his parents. Family lore, however, tells that Bernard had only one sister, Rosa, and that he and his sister were orphaned. There is additional oral history, passed down to his grandchildren, that his mother, whose name was unknown, drowned herself in the Danube after her husband, an army officer, abandoned her and the children. This apparent lie was started nearly a hundred years ago and is believed, now, by some family members despite evidence to the contrary. For many, to let go of long-held beliefs and impressions is difficult. However, the myth has proved to be untrue after careful review of the genealogical records in Salt Lake City as well as marriage records in Vienna. The myth, however, was perpetuated for decades. It appears that the family's pattern of secrecy started when Bernard began to need to be seen in a certain way in order to succeed in Hungarian society. This pattern of secrecy, the formulating of less-than-true stories, and the withholding of information, would continue through the generations.

Prior to August 2012 nobody in the Alexander/Broessler family knew the name of Bernard's parents or that he had siblings other than the mysterious Rosa. Some scholarly articles state Bernard was born in Budapest though a closer review of genealogical archives at The Church of Jesus Christ of Latter Day Saints reveals that he was born just south of Budapest, in the town of Kiskunfelegyhaza. All of his siblings, however, were born in Budapest, or so it seems when researching genealogical records. Contradicting this information is Eva Gabor's assertion in her book titled *Bernat Alexander* that Bernard was born in Godollo, a suburb of Budapest located about twenty miles NW of the city. Interestingly, Lilla, Alexander's youngest sister, mentioned to her daughter Stella that she remembered visits to the town as a child. It is likely that Bernard's family owned land not far from Budapest, and then settled into the city proper during his early school years. Though Budapest was a very class-conscious society, unlike the rest of Hungary, social mobility was possible. It was the possibility of social mobility and a more liberal life that drew many to Budapest and Bernard's parents may have been part of that movement. A recently obtained scanned copy of Bernard's certificate or diploma after completion of his doctorate from Leipzig, in his own handwriting, says he was born in Budapest. Artur Renyi, in his diary describing his life with Bernard's daughter, Borbala, speaks of a farm in Godollo. Eva Gabor writes that Bernard's father owned some land and worked it, farming. Other records uncovered by Raymond Minkus, a professional genealogist and distant cousin, indicate Bernard's father was a merchant in Budapest. What is known is that the family most certainly valued education and learning. Bernard's parents hoped he would become a physician, as noted above, and Bernard himself briefly considered a rabbinical course of study. It is unlikely Bernard's parents were illiterate or poverty-stricken as their firstborn was able to obtain a doctorate degree. That kind of achievement usually does not take place in merely one generation, especially in the 1800s when options for education and travel were significantly more limited than today, especially for Jews.

Bernard and Regina married in Vienna on August 22, 1880 with both their fathers in attendance. The fact that Bernard's father was at the service proves the family story of his being an orphan to be untrue. Bernard's mother died before the wedding took place and, at this time, the exact date is unknown. When the couple wed, Bernard was already a professor of philosophy at the University of Budapest at the young age of thirty. He was one of the leading intellectuals of his time and often met with other philosophers and students in the Budapest cafés. Bernard was a Shakespearean expert, a columnist, and a member of the Hungarian Academy of Sciences. From 1892 he was head of the department of dramaturgy of the Hungarian Academy of Theatre. At the same time, he taught aesthetics and cultural history at the Technical University of Budapest.

During the mid- to late 1800s, in mostly Catholic Eastern Europe, it was the custom to deny one's Jewishness in order to obtain employment, recognition, and acceptance in society, especially in the upper middle class that was largely Catholic. It is possible that Bernard renounced his Jewish heritage in order to obtain a university appointment. Bernard and Regina did not practise Jewish customs or observe the Jewish holidays. Unlike Bernard, however, Regina did not overtly hide or deny her Jewishness. For Bernard, it was inconvenient to be Jewish.

Shortly after the young couple settled into married life, Regina became pregnant with their first child, a daughter and on June 7, 1881 Ilonka was born. Regina sent photos of the toddler, lovingly inscribed to her brother Ignacz Broessler back in Vienna, and life was good for a while. Little Ilonka, as she is referred to now, was scalded in a laundry room accident and died. Her mother gave birth to a second daughter, Erzsebet (Erzsi) on February 1, 1883. Then in September of 1885 Magdalena was born and on January 22, 1891, Ferenc (Franz) was born. Being the first boy after three daughters, and the first child after six years, and it appears the first child conceived after Little Ilonka's death, he always considered himself to be his mother's favorite. In his semiautobiographical book, *The Western Mind in Transition*, Alexander

Dr. Bernard Alexander

describes his mother as the stabilizing factor in the family and the "emotional center" as well. The author wonders if he considered the role of mothers to be the center of the home and that was justification for him to leave the majority of the parenting of his own children to their mother. However, he mentions very little about his mother thereafter

Regina Broessler Alexander on the right, other lady unknown.

and, instead, concentrates on his relationship with his father whom he idolized and called the "Sun King." Inasmuch as Alexander speaks repeatedly about feeling inferior, or not good enough, it may be he was competing with his father for his mother's attention in some oedipal way. Alexander was neither apologetic nor embarrassed about the fact that he idolized his father. His being the first boy played a prominent role in the family dynamics. He would eventually become the most successful child and the only one who could really be compared to the brilliant professor father, Bernard. Ironically, despite his brilliant mind, Alexander speaks repeatedly of his internal conflict caused by an unclear sense of self. He says that working in the field of psychoanalysis offered him the chance to find his true self, his true identity, apart from his father, and allowed him to make connections between his past and present.

Following Alexander, another boy was born, Paul in 1896, followed by a sister Borbala in 1899, and the last child, Lilla, was born in 1902. When Lilla was in her adolescent years, Regina fell ill and Lilla's older sister Erzsi assumed the role of mother to her younger sister as Regina and Bernard travelled to Switzerland for "the cure" and ultimately settled in Germany where Regina entered a nursing home.

The Alexander children's formative years played out in a building that was the local head office of the New York Life Insurance Company. The insurance company occupied the first floor in what is considered to be the lobby in more modern times. Apartments lined the upstairs corridors and overlooked the massive open air courtyard below. The building's architect was Alajos Hauszmann and the building represents a combination of the neoclassical and baroque styles. It is ornate, grand, gilded, and large without being imposing. Ironically, despite its size, it is warm and welcoming. The building was known, then and now, as the New York Palace and is presently a luxury hotel after being extensively renovated by the Italian Boscolo hotel chain. Prior to the Boscolo chain obtaining the building in the early 2000s, it fell into complete disrepair during the years of communism.

The New York Palace sits on the Elizabeth Ring, not far from the Andrassy Blvd., and the Alexanders lived in a large corner apartment on the top floor. It is from a window in this apartment, overlooking the Elizabeth Ring, that Alexander, as a young boy, remembered viewing celebrations for the Hungarian millennium in 1896 and seeing King Franz Josef. It is one of the first memories he mentioned in the beginning of *The Western Mind in Transition*. He was perhaps five years old at the time of these nationwide festivities.

Every cultural advantage was provided for the Alexander children, like the children of the gentry class. Alexander took violin lessons as a child and the romantic Austrian composer Gustav Mahler personally worked with Erszebet, his older sister, who was studying to be an opera singer. She is said to have had a most spectacular soprano voice. At the time Gustav Mahler was the director at the Budapest Opera House. Alexander, who tended to excel at almost everything he attempted, did not like the violin and stopped lessons after a few years. His love of opera, gypsy, and classical music continued throughout his life and he introduced his family to it all.

The building's café, on the ground floor of the New York Life building, was a longtime center of Hungarian literature and poetry since its opening in October of 1894. It was the most beautiful and popular of the cafés in Budapest. Bernard Alexander, then a scholar of Shakespeare as well as a professor of philosophy, met his students and other philosophers in the café while his children and their friends played upstairs in the large marble hallways. The most influential newspapers, many with articles by Bernard, were edited on the building's level known as the gallery. It is rumoured that Nietzsche often attended the café when Bernard was there along with the students, other philosophers, and critics. The café was closed during communist years, reopened, and closed again. After renovations it is again opulent and representative of

New York Palace in late nineteenth century.

the belle époque. One anecdote tells of how the famous writer Ferenc Molnár, on the day the café opened its doors, threw the keys into the Danube thus assuring it would always remain open.

The New York Palace, albeit his family home, had such significance for Alexander that he devoted a separate section to it in his semiauto-biographical work. He wrote with such loving care and attention when describing the New York Palace, that the building almost seems to take on the importance of an actual person for him. Alexander tells of the intellectuals who were neighbors in the apartments and how aristocratic the children of those professors felt when comparing themselves to the children of businessmen. Other professors, the education minister, and a well-known lawyer also called the New York Palace home.

In the Alexander family, it was considered more important to pursue an education and excel in something intellectual or artistic than to be a financial success. This ideal was part of the value system inherent in the very class-conscious society of Budapest. At the end of the nineteenth century workers in finance and business were not considered part of the social elite despite their large incomes. The importance of a liberal education had been instilled in Bernard by his parents. In retrospect, one can see how his son's elitist leanings began to take hold at such an early age of six or seven. Alexander continued to place high significance on academics throughout his entire life and stressed the importance of an education and giving back to others less fortunate. The importance of money, or its meaning in life, was never discussed. And remember, the financially successful, the financial gentry, were neither admired nor considered successful. Ironically, it was important to show a perfect picture to the outside world.

The intellectual society of Budapest clearly played a major role in Alexander's development. Budapest was then one of the major thriving cultural centers in Europe. It was nicknamed the Paris of Eastern Europe. Saturday nights with the Alexander family were stimulating and exciting as writers, professors, journalists, and artists came to the apartment to discuss the latest ideas. The family entertained a lot and was very social. Cultural and political events were the topics discussed by the father and his children as all sat around the dinner table. Dinner was sometimes taken in Alexander's father's library where lively and challenging conversations took place. It is most likely that Regina entertained the wives of the men who attended while Bernard met with the men and discussed important topics of the day and maybe smoked cigars as they enjoyed a demitasse. While Alexander was too young to attend those discussions, he sometimes hid in the hallway in order to eavesdrop on the adult conversations. He was inquisitive and wanted to be as involved as he could be. He was aching to show his father how intelligent he was. He was insecure and unsure of himself as most adolescents are.

It was a time of hope and peace in Europe. It was also a time of opportunity and positivity. It is clear that the Alexander children grew up in a sheltered, elitist, and liberal home. That sheltered and traditional yet politically liberal atmosphere was recreated when Alexander raised his children and again when his oldest daughter, Silvia, raised her daughter with the strong influence of her parents and their upper middle class European values. In the home she shared with him, more than fifty years later, as everyone sat discussing art, languages, and history with Alexander seated at the head of the table, the old class values of early twentieth-century Budapest were kept alive as they influenced thinking then and now.

Alexander and his siblings played with their childhood friends from the building along the marble corridors of the New York Palace. He reveals he would sometimes experience periods of inattention when a youngster. As the sun would shine onto the marble floors, his mind would wander from the childish games. Greatly influenced by his father's thinking and their talks together, Alexander daydreamed about the nature of the world; he mused in the ethereal world. He was his father's son. His father stressed the importance of pure science and hoped that his son would become an archaeologist. It is thought that his father wanted to pursue archaeology and was unable to do so, as written in *The Western Mind in Transition*. According to Eva Gabor in *Bernat Alexander*, Bernard's own parents hoped he would be a physician. It is unknown if this is actually true or part of an elaborate ruse to invent a more interesting family background than being merely the son of a farmer or merchant without high ambitions. It is true that Bernard studied what could be considered medical school courses when attending university, but disliked it. Perhaps he did this to please his parents. Both Bernard and his son did well academically at the gymnasium and Bernard was proud of his son's achievements. Pleasing his father was important to him, just as pleasing him would become important to his children and grandchild. Alexander even tried to study archaeology to please his father but failed miserably and was totally disinterested in it. The desire to please the older generations seems to be a recurring theme in the family, as in many families. In so doing, one obtains attention, praise, a sense of accomplishment, and positive regard.

The family was a very private one. In fact, despite the family's liberal political views, it was fairly old-fashioned and rigid in its traditions, emphasizing an outward appearance of dignity and restraint. Alexander was, too, very private and did not share his feelings and thoughts easily with others. Despite his professional work, his family rarely saw him encourage others to share their feelings either. Even though he could be very private, he did relish being the center of attention and, as a successful analyst, years later, often travelled in the summer months, when on hiatus at the Chicago Institute for Psychoanalysis, with an entourage of students and colleagues. This group may have fulfilled two needs: the need to be adored and the need to be protected, as if by a buffer. In fact, his cousin, Judith Revesz-Laqueur, said that despite feeling comfortable to visit her many times, "He was a hard man to know." Indeed, it is through the stories of family members, former colleagues, and friends, and after reading countless documents, that a truer sense of the man has emerged. Not the idealized and idolized grandfather of a childhood, but as the respected adult he was. He has at last become real and no longer perfect.

The Alexanders and Broesslers travelled together even when the children were in their late teens, and in old family photographs they can even be seen together on holidays as adults. Family vacations were taken to the Black Sea or to the French Riviera, to Switzerland to ski or to Vienna to see extended family. One of Alexander's favorite vacations was when the entire family travelled by train with his uncle Ignacz and his family. Ignacz Broessler, his mother's favorite brother, an industrialist and businessman, was more practical than his ethereal father, Bernard. During these family trips, his uncle treated Bernard like an absentminded professor while handling problems encountered during the journeys. The young Alexander admired these practical attributes and in so doing began to see his own father as less perfect and all-knowing. This change in his thinking about his father is discussed in his book *The Western Mind in Transition*. The change in the author's perception of Alexander did not happen until a much later time.

Being a good student, Alexander excelled in languages, philosophy, and history, and in his later school years his interests included mathematics and physics, which may have been the beginning of his so-called rebellion or rejection of his father's wishes for his future. When he finished his studies at the gymnasium, he was theoretically free to choose any area of study. However, this freedom of choice was strongly influenced by Bernard, who wanted his son to study the classics, and the need of the son to please his father. This wish of the father may have been unspoken though no less understood. During the last years of study at the gymnasium, Alexander discussed his future goals with his uncle Ignacz who was dead set against his nephew pursuing the humanities. He tried to encourage his nephew to study something different and gave him books on physics and on philosophy by Ernst Mach, who would influence his future thinking. Father and son had numerous discussions about the pros and cons of philosophy vs. science. Most certainly Bernard believed his son was neglecting his traditional studies as he continued to focus more on the natural sciences at school.

At the age of eighteen, in 1909, Alexander enrolled at the University of Gottingen for a summer semester: the same university where his father had studied years before. He would attend the Café National in that city. Eventually he decided to study medicine, a choice that initially caused his father to feel great disappointment. His choice to attend his father's alma mater may have been an attempt to defuse his father's initial negative reaction to his decision to study medicine. At Gottingen he studied with Professors Max Verworn and George Elias Mueller. In Professor Mueller's laboratory, Alexander met Geza Revesz, the Hungarian psychologist who first introduced industrial psychology to the world, and who later became a brother-in-law after marrying his older sister Magda in 1910.

After just a semester at Gottingen, Alexander returned to Budapest to continue his university education. He was given a microscope by his cousin Gustav Broessler to help with his medical studies. Alexander would, years later, with the help of his sister Borbala, provide his cousin Gustav with a letter of support to assist with his emigration to America after WWII.[1]

When Alexander was a young medical student, his father gave him a copy of Freud's *The Interpretation of Dreams* to read. The professor father was then the editor of the *Journal of Philosophy* and a new edition of Freud's book had been sent to him. He said to his firstborn son, in a note attached to the book, "This belongs in your field. It is not philosophy. Read it and write a review" (Alexander, 1960). Alexander said in his semiautobiographical work that he returned the book to his

---

[1]Eva Broessler Weissman, the daughter of Gustav Broessler, is the first cousin the author met in 2010, of the family kept from her by her grandparents and her mother. She wrote *The War Came to Me* in 2009 and died March 2, 2013.

father with the comments that the work was not philosophy, nor was it medicine. Both father and son thought the book was crazy. That was Alexander's first encounter with the field of psychoanalysis and with Freud. He would later discuss the unconscious with his father and tell his father it could help him to better understand Shakespeare. Years were to pass, though, before that discussion would take place. And a change in Alexander's mind would take place as well. That was one of his most important characteristics, an open and brilliant mind. He got both from his father.

As a result of his work in Gottingen, with Mueller and Verworn, Alexander developed an interest in how biology affects the body and mind, sort of the crude beginnings of psychosomatic theory. His detailed discussions with his father about philosophy, from an early age, clearly influenced his thought. In his third year of studies, Alexander worked with Franz Tangl, a Hungarian physician and pathologist who was, by the 1910s, a professor at the Hungarian Academy of Sciences. As part of the work in the laboratory with Professor Tangl, together with Geza Revesz, Alexander performed various experiments on dogs regarding oxygen consumption and blood flow to the brain. This study was a continuation of his obsession with the mind-body connection which would further consume his thinking for years. He cites this as his second foray into the field of psychoanalysis though he continued to describe himself still as an "obsessed lab worker." This work resulted in his first academic paper and it was published before he completed medical school.

Even after this success in the lab, Alexander tells in his autobiography of still being a disappointment to his father. Feeling disappointment, real or imagined, was not new to Alexander and these feelings plagued him his entire life. He remembered the busts of the old masters and Greeks looking down on him from atop the ceiling-high bookcases in his father's study. He said they looked disappointed. Those busts are, indeed, imposing and perhaps in the midst of a heated discussion with his father, may have appeared to show disappointment and disapproval. The same busts now sit atop those same bookcases in Alexander's niece's home in Malcesine, Italy. Bernard's bookcases continue to hold the professor father's treasured books, hundreds of them, a century later. To experience that perceived disappointment must have been crushing to him as he already felt not good enough and appears to have been vulnerable to criticism. It is sad that this feeling of insecurity and not measuring up would haunt him with almost dogged determination in spite of his unparalleled successes. In fact, one of his longtime colleagues and a former student, as well as family friend, Dr. Hedda Bolgar, often spoke of his insecurity and his need for reassurance after he gave a well-received lecture.

Bernard Alexander had little interest in experimental psychology, the field his son was expressing interest in. He told his son repeatedly that it seemed improbable to understand a horse by counting its hairs. He was interested in ethereal issues and not in pure science. It seems that the elder Alexander would have preferred that his son be more interested in the essential problems of mankind and less interested in oxygen consumption and blood gases. In that, the professor father was a man of his time, an educated snob interested only in intellectual pursuits during the waning days of the Habsburg era. He was simply not a practical man.

On March 1, 1912, while still studying medicine, Alexander was drafted into the Hungarian Army for six months. He was able to complete his medical education in November of 1913. He was, however, undecided about his long-term future career path, yet knew he was not destined to spend his entire professional life in a laboratory. After graduation from medical school he began to work at the Budapest Institute for Health, and in April 1914 he was again conscripted into military service and was stationed at a military hospital in Budapest. On June 28, 1914, when the heir to the throne of the Austro-Hungarian Empire, Franz Ferdinand and his wife, Sophie, were assassinated, war was declared and changed the course of his life; the war took him away from his family and his Budapest, and introduced him to challenges not considered before.

Politics, and the impact of political change, previously only discussed around the dinner table or in the professor father's study, changed the family forever. Alexander would never again return to the New York Palace. His brothers and sisters, with their various pursuits, had already left Budapest or would scatter as a consequence of the Great War. All would leave Budapest except one, Borbala. Her decision to remain behind, during the days between the two World Wars, and after, will ultimately open a Pandora's box for future generations to discover. A Pandora's box of confusion and secrets with only some answers provided. One thing was certain. The opulent, safe, and intellectual life at the Palace, so enjoyed by Alexander in this special family, was over.

CHAPTER THREE

The Great War and meeting nobility

At the time the Great War broke out in 1914, the Austro-Hungarian Empire, which comprised nearly 700,000 square kilometres, had a population of 52 million and almost half lived in Hungary. This empire was considered to be one of the great powers in Europe. The prime minister hesitated to enter the war after the assassinations of the crown prince and his wife and only agreed to war when Germany promised to neutralize Romania and also promised that no Serbian territory would be annexed to the empire.

The military forces of the Austro-Hungarian Empire remained relatively unified during the war despite their multiethnic nature, and proved to be reliable and were used on the front lines. Alexander's service, however, began on hospital train Number 38 travelling between Budapest and Vienna, though he would eventually see battle on the Italian front.

Hospital trains replaced horse-drawn ambulances as soon as rail service was established throughout Europe in the middle of the nineteenth century. This method of military medicine included the evacuating, distributing, and treating of the wounded and presented a massive transportation challenge. During World War I the usage of hospital trains was an important element in the planning for battles. Initially the trains were converted passenger cars and eventually specialized mobile hospitals were built. Although these outfitted ambulance trains were sometimes stationed at the front, the typical pattern was for them to carry equipment and soldiers to battle and return with the wounded.

After two years of service, Alexander was promoted to the rank of senior physician and given the Gold Medal for Bravery after injuring his elbow. It is unknown how the injury occurred. He recuperated in Salzburg and soon thereafter rejoined his regiment. He considered these war years to be adventurous and he is said to have often spoken of them with fondness to others, but never to his children or others in the family. In fact, during the research for this work, it was discovered through the help of a cousin in Brno, Czech Republic, that he was indeed injured. This information was not known previously by the family.

Those first two years of the war were Alexander's first real time away from home for any prolonged period. He had been away, in various

Dr. Franz Alexander during WWI aboard hospital train.

cities, for medical school, and had always returned to his beloved
Budapest. But leaving to go to war was different and Budapest meant
home, security, and family. As an officer and a physician, he was treated
with respect and admiration. Good manners always fit into his sense
of elitism, and during his formative years, professors and others in
authority positions were treated with respect. However, the final years
of the war were different and difficult for him: not so civilized. He was
then stationed on the Italian front for the Battles of the Isonzo throughout most of 1917. These were a series of twelve engagements between
Hungarian forces and the Italian Army. These battles occurred between
June 1915 and November 1917 and took place along the Isonzo River
on the eastern side of the Italian front, what is now Slovenia and Italy.
Because Italy had signed the secret Treaty of London, in April 1915,
which committed her to an invasion of Austria in return for Allied
promises of Habsburg territory, the Austro-Hungarians were forced to
move some of their forces from the Eastern Front and the war in the
mountains began.

With the exit of Russia from the war in 1917, Austria-Hungary
devoted significant forces to the Italian Front and received reinforce-
ments from their German allies. The Austro-Hungarian emperor
reached an agreement with the Germans to undertake a new offensive
against Italy, a move supported by both the chief of the general staff,
Arz von Straussenburg and the commander of the South Tyrolean Army
Group, Conrad von Hötzendorf. In the autumn of 1917, at the Battles
of Caporetto and Longarone, the Germans and Austrians defeated the
Italians who fell back to the Piave River.

It was during this tumultuous time that Alexander met Anita Venier
(she was Anna Ida Venier at birth and changed her name to Anita when
she was granted US citizenship). Annie, as he referred to her, was set to
become a nun and when she met her future husband, she was about to
take her final vows. Blonde and blue-eyed, with patrician beauty, she
was indeed a striking figure; the total opposite of Alexander who was
short, stout, and very dark, with brown hair and eyes.

It is said that Anita Venier's lineage is one of nobility. She claimed
to be descended from the House of Venier which established itself in
Venice in the fourteenth century. Genealogical records can be traced
back to Anita's great-great-grandfather Cristoforo Venier who was
born in 1781 (the four times great-grandfather of the author), but not
all records are complete. Her ancestors included two doges, Antonio

Venier and Sebastiano Venier, and her mother's family, from Padua, came from the old established house of Cherubini. Her parents were Count Carlo Venier and Guiseppina Cherubini, perhaps married in the late 1800s. One thing is clear: her father died in a duel before she was born in March of 1894. Annie took a remnant of the bullet that killed her father and encased it in gold to make a ring. She passed the ring on to her daughter, Silvia, who kept it for safekeeping for decades before passing it on to her firstborn daughter, Ilonka. It is one small tangible link to the past and to a maternal great-grandfather.

When Annie was only three years of age, her mother placed her in a convent school for children of noble families as was the custom at the time; she was thus "given to the church" and not expected to marry. The Ancelle di Gesu Bambino was founded by Elena Silvestri in 1884. This school's initial location was in Venice and later the young girl went to live at one of the convent's newer sites in Gorizia near the Udine region of northern Italy. The convent, sponsored by Baroness Maria von Spaun, was aristocratic and poor. Baroness von Spaun was the sister of an Austrian naval hero, Baron Hermann von Spaun. The baron married a woman from Trieste and the family became well acquainted with the local area including Gorizia. While this information cannot be substantiated by Vatican records, it can be surmised to be true from many of Annie's paintings depicting village life in the areas near Gorizia and Udine as well as information about Alexander's deployment during World War I. Annie spoke of the Baroness Spaun in a mid-1930s interview and the Vatican confirmed that the nuns, to this day, are referred to as the "Sisters Spaun." It is unclear what the relationship was with her mother, especially as a very young child, but it is known the family trauma of being separated from her mother no doubt had psychological sequelae. Most would later describe Annie as "the difficult one" and it is easy to understand why with such a challenging childhood.

The mother superior and foundress of the convent was an artist of some reputation and many of her paintings hung in convents throughout Italy. Annie said the mother superior recognized her artistic talents and took her under her wing at a very young age. The youngster was allowed to mix paints and assist the mother superior when she was painting. Paints were considered a luxury and the colors needed for a painter's palette were not always available. The paint mixing technique was rather crude: stale coffee grounds were used for browns and shoe polish helped to create black.[1] In order to make additional colors, the mother superior and her little protégé mixed ground flower petals with linseed oil. Many of Annie's early works reflect this religious influence, depicting nuns in dark and muted tones, performing various tasks around the convent, as well as the gardens of the convent and local towns.

Soon Annie was allowed to graduate from mixing colors to painting with them on canvas under the watchful eye of the mother superior who later called in the painter Enrico Rossini to give her lessons. As the convent was for females only, he, as the only male, was required to enter through the main entrance. He carried umbrellas all the time and Annie nicknamed him "the man with big umbrellas." When he came to give instruction, he set up an umbrella as if the legs of an easel. The child thought the legs were additional umbrellas. Lessons took place in the gardens of the convent and he introduced her to watercolors. She was soon painting trees and flowers found in the gardens. When Annie was fourteen years old she was given her first box of paints as a birthday present. When she ultimately left the convent school, she took with her memories of the solemn, silent, dark spaces within the religious walls. Despite the influence of the gayer colors of Rossini, she had been more influenced by the sombre and depressing browns and blacks used primarily by the mother superior, and her work reflected that influence for many years.

As the Hungarian Army came over the Alps into northern Italy, during the Battles of the Izonso and Piave Rivers, and invaded the areas near Venice and the Veneto, Annie volunteered as a Red Cross worker, providing help to the nurses and doctors caring for the injured. It was most common for women to volunteer as nurses despite no formal training. She sometimes travelled on the hospital trains as part of her service as a volunteer. She was living in the Accende di Gesu Bambino in Gorizia, Italy and about to take her final vows. She became gravely ill with tuberculosis and, as the others fled the approaching Hungarians in fear, she stayed behind when the convent was evacuated. Alexander chose the convent as a good location for his field hospital. Family lore is that he saved her life and she fell in love with him almost immediately.

------

[1]Before the advent of sophisticated hair dyes, Annie used stale coffee grounds to add color to her naturally pale blonde hair.

The story goes something like this: She was unconscious but when he approached her, trying to assess her medical condition, she was suddenly conscious and looked up into his eyes, and fell in love. He did, in fact, nurse her to health. Like an ending in a true Hollywood movie, they were married as soon as she was able to travel. In marrying an Italian Catholic woman of noble heritage, Alexander had certainly "married up" and thus, unwittingly, began his own metamorphosis into something other than an Eastern European Jew. Her aristocratic ancestry, as well as his denial of his Jewish heritage, no doubt allowed them to ultimately move about Chicago's high society with ease.

After the collapse of the front along the River Piave in November 1918, and the official end of World War I, Alexander returned to Hungary to be demobilized. On his journey he was crammed into a cattle car along with dozens of unruly sailors who tore off his uniform badges and mocked him. He was accustomed to the civility of officers around him, and to the elite and cultured world of his prewar young adulthood, and was not prepared for the barbarous antics of the sailors. It was a most unpleasant experience for him.

When Alexander left Italy, his new bride remained behind in the area of the Italian Alps and the Dolomites and contact between them was minimal. It was a period of political unrest and revolution and the newlyweds were unable to communicate for quite some time. There was chaos everywhere. Through the efforts of his parents and his younger brother, Paul, all of whom fled to Switzerland, Alexander and Annie were ultimately reunited in Berlin where he would begin his studies in psychoanalysis. In mid-1920, Annie would become pregnant with their first daughter, Silvia.

Postwar Europe was in shambles. The loss for Hungary was a complete loss. The Austro-Hungarian Empire broke apart and Hungary lost two thirds of its possessions. Eight million Hungarians were left in Hungary and more than three million Hungarians were stranded outside of the newly established borders. New nations, such as Czechoslovakia, Poland, and the Balkan state known as the Kingdom of Serbs, Croats and Slovenes were established while Italy and Romania extended their borders. Hungary lost its most southern regions to Yugoslavia. Bosnia-Herzegovina was also incorporated into Yugoslavia and Croatia became part of Yugoslavia also, breaking a 900-year relationship with Hungary.

The euphoria and idealism infecting most Hungarians prior to and during World War I ended abruptly. It was a devastating defeat. There was widespread disillusionment. Having seen the senseless loss of human life and the negative consequences of war up close, Alexander became disillusioned as well. It was as if the war, its eventual change into the cold war, the loss of personal freedoms, and the resultant emergence of paranoia, put an end to his naïve and sheltered life. His Budapest, one of opulence, political liberalism, scholarly debates, literature, and the arts, servants, and opportunity, was gone. Hungary was about to enter an era of prolonged darkness and political and social upheaval as communism and violence loomed on the horizon. During this time, Jews in most of Europe were regarded with fear. A new kind of hatred emerged as post-World War I nationalism became strong, especially among the younger generation. It was a kind of pseudo-nationalism bordering on fascism. It is as if the liberal changes that occurred in the mid-1800s were no longer considered viable, as this new, aggressive form of nationalism, not to be confused with patriotism, was taking hold. Jews were regarded as aliens and even those who had converted to Catholicism, like the Alexanders, were labelled Jewish in terms of their sentiments and beliefs. People were afraid. And when people are afraid, as political change occurs around them, they begin to hate. The Jews in Europe, and particularly in Austria and Hungary, who had been assimilated after the political liberalism in the 1870s and as an aftermath of the Compromise, were now hated. Hatred can be more damaging than fear, though fear may linger longer. The effects of hatred and fear will touch the lives of the Alexander children. Happily, Alexander would live to see his beloved Hungary begin to emerge from the darkness, but it would take decades.

Immediately after the Armistice, Alexander returned to Budapest and began his work with Professor Erno Emil Moravcsik at the Budapest Department of Psychiatry and Neurology. Professor Moravcsik's lab was attached to the university. In addition to working in the laboratory, Alexander's responsibilities included inpatient work with psychiatric patients. At this time of his professional development, he steered clear of psychological interpretations and was primarily interested in the biology of psychiatry. He states that blood chemistry was his only true passion at the time. He is said to have not been interested in his patients' personality structure at all during these years. As a mental health professional herself, and knowing the impact Freud had on his theoretical orientation, the author considers it odd to know of his initial disinterest in interpretation. Indeed, the timing was not right and he was not ready to embark on his own personal journey of discovery which allowed him to commit to psychoanalysis.

As a medical student Alexander read Freud's *The Interpretation of Dreams* and left it for his father to read as well. Both father and son, at that time, considered this work not to be medicine. Now, working for the hospital in Budapest, one of Alexander's psychiatric patients, a schizophrenic, awoke from a period of catatonia, and he wanted to talk repeatedly about his dreams. Alexander remembered Freud's work and thought, "This book is crazy and the patient is crazy." He thought, "Maybe this crazy book will help me understand this crazy patient," and began to use it to help him understand this man's dreams. He also wondered who should handle such patients and whether or not psychoanalysis may be of some help. He reread the important book and met a woman psychiatrist who would influence him greatly. She was a pupil of Freud and was working in the hospital. Alexander viewed her as poised, intelligent, and the only one who truly understood the patients. Despite being impressed with her skills, he was not yet convinced that psychoanalysis was right for him.

Alexander read and reread Freud's works, finding them, at times, tedious and painful to follow with their vague and ambiguous concepts. He was more accustomed to the literary-influenced philosophical works shared and discussed with his father, followed by years spent in a lab working with pure science. Finally, after poring over the works, time and time again, he began to have an understanding of the concepts and the etiology of kleptomania. Although welcomed by the local Freudians as a potential convert, Alexander still retreated from the group and from making a commitment to the field.

As he studied, again and again, the psychoanalytic literature of the time, it began to make sense to Alexander. It was as if he had not fully understood the concepts earlier when discussing them with his father. Or perhaps a period of independence, when away during the war, allowed him to consider views not popular with his father. He voraciously read and reread all the current writings and came to believe this new technique could help his patients. It was then that he realized he had to abandon his hopes of an academic career and accept the fact he would disappoint his father once again. Alexander began to understand that the distance between his father's thinking and his own interests could not be bridged. The giving up of this unachievable goal was energizing for him and made him happy.

In the early 1910s, prior to World War I, Sandor Ferenczi and others founded the Budapest Psychoanalytic Society. Soon Alexander was invited to attend but he rejected the invitation. Again, he could not make a commitment. He could not endorse the society's condemnation of academic psychiatry. He found himself with a dilemma: To endorse psychoanalysis meant most likely an end to his laboratory work and a denial of his father's rejection of psychoanalysis. "The practice of psychoanalysis was simply a horror in the eyes of the philosopher father …" (Alexander, 1960, p. 55). He was still keen on impressing his father and his father had already sensed a competition between the two. The war, ironically, and the images that were encountered by Alexander were what eventually allowed him to appreciate the psychology of the unconscious.

As the new Hungarian political changes unfolded, post-World War I, so too did politics ultimately bring change for the Alexander family. The Hungary of the Alexander children's youth no longer existed. As communism began to emerge as a presence, a student of his father's, the new Minister of Education, discharged the professor father who then lost his academic appointment and his prestigious standing in the Hungarian Academy of Sciences. It is written that Bernard lost his appointment, his professorship, and his pension because of alleged support of a proletarian dictatorship in 1919. After Bernard lost his academic appointment he did not respond to the allegations made against him. The first time Alexander saw his father cry was when he disclosed this information to his wife and children. Bernard was deeply hurt to lose his academic standing and only after his wife's death in August of 1922 did he return to Hungary. It was months later that he moved back into his former home, a corner apartment at 24 Belgrade Street, overlooking the Elizabeth Bridge, with his daughter Borbala, a photographer, and her husband Artur Renyi, a mechanical engineer and linguist. He did not apply for public posts but lived in partial seclusion and isolation. He wrote for newspapers and magazines to earn money. Later Gyula Kornis, president of the Hungarian Academy of Science, and his former students helped Bernard get his pension reinstated. Bernard's daughter Borbala worked tirelessly for three years to restore her father's excellent academic reputation. With some money coming into the household,

Belgrade Street overlooking Danube River at Elizabeth Bridge.

Bernard could then return to writing without the worry and pressure of earning money. He wrote about Spinoza, Petőfi (Hungarian poet of the 1848–49 revolution), Madách (Hungarian drama writer), and Michelangelo.

Alexander left his beloved Budapest for Vienna in 1919, where he remained for almost a year, and was eventually reunited with his bride in Berlin. It was in Berlin that he would continue his journey, both personal and professional. Alexander again was demoralized and depressed. His father had been stripped of his prestigious university appointment and his standing in the community. The family home at the New York Palace had been abandoned years before as the children went their separate ways. For Alexander, as well as his siblings, everything was different and about to change even more dramatically. The life shared and experienced, with his family all together and prosperous, would never again be seen or felt.

This time of chaos and change would constitute the beginning of the making of who he would become. It was the beginning of the separation between his private self and his public self. The importance of the public persona would develop. It was also the beginning of the scattering of the Alexanders, and the family would not again be truly connected for almost 100 years. All hell had broken out in Hungary and in the family, too. By then Magda and Erzsi were gone, Paul and Lilla were soon to go to Berlin, and Feri would be in Berlin too. Only Borka remained in Budapest. When Borka warned cousins in Vienna, in the late 1930s, to evacuate because of Hitler, she still chose to remain in Budapest. Nobody knows why and her husband's diary does not provide a clue. That mystery will remain forever unsolved.

CHAPTER FOUR

The Alexander children in the twentieth century

In order to fully understand Franz Alexander, it is important to be exposed to a comprehensive description of the Alexander siblings, their challenges, and their accomplishments. The family created by Bernard Alexander and Regina Broessler was a close-knit family and private, though paradoxically, they were all extremely social. They were charismatic, charming, and attractive to others. Their circle of friends was large and diverse and all were extremely well educated and sophisticated and included artists, musicians, philosophers, and educators.

Just one year after their marriage, a first daughter, Little Ilonka, was born. Two more daughters followed, Erzsebet and Magdalena, and then a first son, Ferenc. Another daughter Borbala was followed by Paul, a second son, and the youngest child, Lillian, was born in 1902.

During these years the family lived in the New York Palace on the Elizabeth Ring in District Seven on the Pest side of the Danube river. District Seven is known to be the Jewish section of Budapest. Both Regina and Bernard came from Jewish backgrounds yet their children were baptized Roman Catholic as was the custom in upper middle class academic circles. Interestingly, this information of a Jewish heritage is absent from Alexander's semi-autobiographical work *The Western Mind in Transition* and his oldest daughter, Silvia, died in 2003 without knowing this fact. This clue to a Jewish heritage seems to be of interest to all; every cousin met over the last five years, soon after meeting would ask, almost in hushed tones, "When did you find out you were Jewish?" It is as if everyone is obsessed with this information, the keeping of the secret, and the exposing of the secret, and has been for some time, too. The Alexander children were not raised Jewish. Only one sibling, and her descendants, would embrace the Jewish faith and in so doing, their heritage as well. The rest, upon learning the truth, would continue as if nothing had changed. The knowledge of a heritage denied would have little meaning for them.

Ilonka Alexander

Not much is known about Little Ilonka other than her date of birth in 1881 and her date of death in 1885. She is known to have died from extensive burns as a result of a laundry accident involving scalding hot water in the basement of the family's apartment building, presumably the New York Palace, which was completed in 1884. There are two remaining photographs taken in Budapest by a Hungarian photographer, most likely taken on her second and third birthdays. Both photographs are lovingly inscribed from Regina to her favorite brother, Ignacz. When this author met Alexander's sister's and Geza Revesz's daughter, Judith Laqueur-Revesz, a cousin, in 2010, she presented her with the photos of Little Ilonka. The author feels a strong connection to this little girl who died too young so many years ago and after whom she was named.

* * *

Shortly after the author's birth in late 1944, her parents separated and her mother returned to live with her own parents in Chicago on the shore of Lake Michigan. She had been sharing a small apartment on Ridgewood Court in the Hyde Park section of Chicago, close to the university, with her husband George Rotariu. This marriage probably was doomed from the start. Silvia, Alexander's firstborn, was raised in a privileged manner, with money and servants, private schools and trips abroad and most likely was not prepared for life as the wife of a struggling graduate student who had two jobs and little time to spend with her. She was accustomed to getting what she wanted and he had

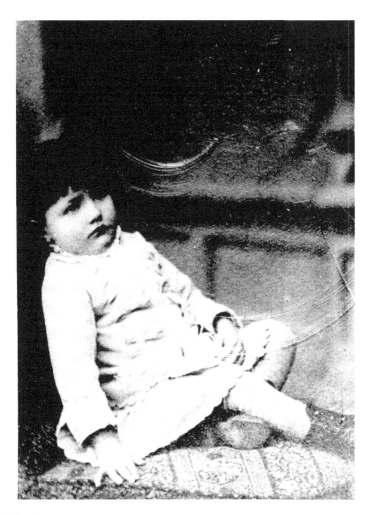

Little Ilonka

little time to cater to her needs though it is clear he loved her dearly. Both mother and father were the children of immigrants; however, their lives had been distinctly different. When the marriage eventually disintegrated, it seemed most natural that Silvia would return to her parents, the author's grandparents, Big Mama and Big Papa.

Ilonka had not yet been baptized and her parents had named her Nina Alexandra Rotariu at birth. As Alexander did not approve of his daughter's choice of husband, a struggling graduate student at the University of Chicago, and the marriage was ending, he is alleged to have said he wanted to name his granddaughter after his sister and himself. When he did that, he took charge of her life. He effectively wiped out any reference to Ilonka's (Nina's) father and let his own daughter Silvia know she could not even name her own daughter properly. Alexander then issued an edict in the family that neither his daughter nor his wife was to ever mention George Rotariu again in the presence of his granddaughter. The family would then refer to Ilonka's father as George #1 as Silvia had married her third husband who also was named George #2. Alexander would nickname his daughter Silvia "the marrying kind", a line from her favorite movie, *Now, Voyager*.

Alexander called George Rotariu a year later after the divorce in 1945, when Silvia was engaged to marry a second time. He informed him that this new husband, Douglas Nigel Thomas, wanted to adopt Ilonka and that he thought this adoption should be allowed to take place. Alexander spoke to Ilonka's father about assuring a stable environment in which for her to grow and develop with this new father, who was called her "Thomas father." Alexander offered a bribe to the biological father of $50,000 in order to stay away and not interfere in her life. George turned him down and said if Dr. Alexander thought it best, he would stay away. When Ilonka met her biological father, years later, he rationalized and explained his nonexistent role in her life: "… because your grandfather was an expert. He must have known what was best." Ilonka never learned of the $50,000 offer until she was almost fifty years old when her Aunt Vicki revealed the secret. Throughout the years, until his death in 2010, George would often say, "But I am not your legal father." It seems this legal technicality gave him the justification he needed for his many decisions to not become involved or be responsible for his daughter's upbringing. It is clear, however, that he was devastated when Silvia left him. When cleaning out Vicki's home in 2002, a song written by George after the marriage broke up was found among her possessions. The song is full of sadness and regret. It was a surprise, and a door to the past, and how he felt so long ago about his first wife and infant daughter. George would become a world-famous nuclear physicist and died in 2010, just one month shy of his ninety-third birthday.

Erzsebet Alexander (Gyorgy, Major)

Erzsebet was born on 1 February 1883 in Budapest. Like another Alexander sister, she was not particularly beautiful but was striking in appearance. She was formidable and strong, physically as well as mentally. Erzsebet was known as Erzsi and studied voice as a youngster in the hopes of being an opera star. She is said to have had a beautiful soprano voice. The family often attended performances at the Hungarian Opera House and the director of the orchestra provided private lessons for the children over the years. As a talented singer she, according to her niece Judith Laqueur, made her concert debut at the age of eighteen, accompanied on the piano by none other than Hungary's most famous musician of the twentieth century, Béla Bartók. Another cousin, Stella Moore remembers that her mother Lilla told her that Bartók was often in the Alexander home and that she (Lilla) would climb under the piano and try to play with the pedals while Bartók made music.

Erzsebet married her first husband, Dr. Miklos Gyorgy, in 1904 and soon thereafter their daughter Edith was born in 1906. The marriage between Miklos and Erzsi was an abusive one and Erzsi left her husband, divorced him, and married Henry Major, a well-known Hungarian painter. Henry Major was Jewish and went to great lengths to conceal his ethnicity as was most important in early twentieth-century Hungary. It is not surprising he would marry a woman whose family concealed their Jewish ethnicity as well. According to the National Portrait Gallery his surname was "Markberieter" and Henry changed his name to Henrik Major very early, perhaps as early as 1910. Artur Renyi, married to another Alexander sister, says in his diary that Henry was more than a decade younger than Erzsi.

The couple, along with Erzsi's daughter, Edith, moved to Paris for a short time in the early 1920s. During this period, Erzsi attempted to regain her extraordinary singing voice, to no avail. It is said among family members that Erzsi screamed so loud during childbirth that she lost her singing voice. That is most likely not true. The Alexander family enjoyed making up stories in order to make themselves look and appear more interesting to outsiders. Erzsi actually believed her singing difficulties resulted from the lack of proper training and her firm conviction, at the time, that she knew everything she needed to know

Erzsebet Major, Lilla (Lillian) von Saher and her children Tibor Alexander and Stella outside the St. Regis Hotel in New York City mid 1940s.

about singing and eschewed formal lessons. For a while Erzsi helped others regain their voice and she moved from France, to Holland, and to Germany. The couple then sailed to America in 1923 and settled in New York City where they had a large apartment with a studio for Henry located in the back. This apartment was across the street from Carnegie Hall. Henry also did a lot of work in ceramics. Stella recalls one ashtray in the form of Hitler's head. You could lay your cigarette sideways in the hair and stub it out in the nose.

Erzsi and Henry moved to southern California where Erzsi found a fertile field of voices to make over, thus allowing silent screen stars with awkward speaking voices to transition smoothly into the new talking motion pictures. The voice transformer, as she was called, worked fourteen to eighteen hour days. She certainly inherited a strong work ethic from her professor father and shared that characteristic with most of her siblings. Erzsi worked with Norma Shearer, Gloria Swanson, and other popular stars. King Vidor, who later would suggest that Alexander's daughter, Silvia, could be a screen sensation like Sonja Henie, sent starlets to Erzsi for help and he, himself, learned how to shout, thanks to her. King Vidor thought he could be more effective on a movie set if he could yell louder. She was well respected among her pupils and believed that many, not just Americans, had problems with their speaking voices. In order to speak more clearly three essential elements were needed: the ability to relax, to breathe rhythmically, and to relax the jaw. Erzsi believed if you could learn to relax the body, you could develop your voice to be a pleasant vehicle to express your thoughts and feelings.

Henry did caricatures of Hollywood stars and covered important courtroom trials as well, when his drawings appeared in the newspapers alongside columns describing the trials. He collaborated with noted sportswriter Bugs Baer and produced over 200 caricatures of Hollywood giants of the time and compiled them into a book, *Hollywood*, published in 1938 with only 800 copies. At least one copy remains in the family. He covered the Lindberg kidnapping case in 1935. As an aside, after Alexander and his wife moved to Chicago, and as an aftermath of the Lindberg kidnapping, Annie is said to have been fearful that her daughters would be kidnapped. Henry also sold many of his works to *The New Yorker* magazine and had various showings in New York City art galleries.

Erzsi thought that "... anyone can sing and have a good speaking voice. Everybody should both sing and speak well." Of course she did not mean that everyone could have a singing career. She believed that singing and speaking worked in tandem and were basic skills to be learned. She felt that singing was as important as reading. "Singing is the most perfect self-expression, the revelation of our inner selves. Good singing is joy, happiness, relief. It gives the sensation of freeing oneself from all earthly bonds." She considered Americans to be lazy with pronunciation and she may have been correct.

After some time, Erzsebet and Henry became dissatisfied with California, most likely because true success did not come to them despite their Hollywood connections and hard work. This inability to turn advantage into fortune would befall others of the Alexander children. Erzsi and Henry returned to the east coast and settled in New York. By the early 1930s, Erzsi's brother, Alexander, had immigrated to America and soon thereafter, the youngest sibling, Lilla, sailed to America too. This left only Borbala in Hungary. For reasons unknown, Borbala, nicknamed Borka, was never mentioned to Alexander's descendants. It is as if her existence was also erased by him as he had erased his granddaughter's father from her life. For Alexander, appearance was most important.

As Stella tells it, one of Erzsi's success stories centered on Desi Halban (Desiree Goudstikker Halban), the daughter of the world famous Austrian soprano Selma Kurz and a concert singer in her own right, known for her interpretations of Mahler with both the New York and Vienna Philharmonic. Several years later Desi married Stella's father, August von Saher. Of interest is the fact that Desi's daughter-in-law, Marei, married to her only son, Edo, won a large settlement as reparations for art stolen during the Second World War. In February 2006 the Dutch government returned over 200 paintings to Marei von Saher. The artwork was looted by the Nazis when Jacques Goudstikker fled the Netherlands, and ended up in museums and galleries located in more than twelve countries, including the United States.

Henry continued to paint and Erzsi worked giving speech lessons. Henry was embraced by the artist colony of Provincetown on Cape Cod where he spent summers for most of the 1930s and 1940s until his death. He loved the dunes, the beach, and the loneliness of the Cape. He lived on the Cape with Dr. Clara Thompson and they began a fourteen-year affair. It was as if he and Erzsi had an understanding: When summer came around each year he travelled to Provincetown and lived with Dr. Thompson. When the summer ended, he returned to New York to live with his wife. It seems as though both women accepted the arrangement.

Ironically, Henry's long-time lover, Clara Thompson, was a professional foe of Alexander. She belonged to a group of analysts who supported research and understanding based on direct observation as opposed to the Freudian method of abstract interpretation of the unconscious. She worked closely with Erich Fromm, Karen Horney, with whom Alexander had a disappointing professional relationship in Chicago, Erik Erikson and others and made considerable contributions to the field of psychoanalysis. One wonders what, or if any, conversations occurred between Dr. Thompson and Alexander. Interestingly, however, Alexander was not so far from accepting many of Thompson's ideas inasmuch as he fully supported research and ultimately conducted research to study the effectiveness of the therapeutic relationship in psychoanalysis. Such research required, above all, direct observation.

The affair between Clara Thompson and Henry Major continued until the summer of 1948. Eventually Erzsi obtained a divorce and wanted to get the final papers signed by Henry. She was driving down to Cape Cod, with some friends, when a bee or wasp flew into the car. She was distracted and started to swat at the intruder. Erzsi lost control of the car and crashed into a tree. She died from her injuries and others in the car were hurt as well, though recovered. She died on August 27, 1948 and less than a month later Henry died in Provincetown in the home of his lover, Clara Thompson. He was only 59 years old. Erich Fromm gave the eulogy and Henry was buried in the local cemetery. Alexander attended the funeral of his brother in law. Ten years later Dr. Thompson died and she was buried alongside Henry.

* * *

In 1986 the author was working as a clinical social worker for the West Los Angeles Veterans Administration Hospital and received a call to interview for a job at the Boston VA Medical Center. She was interviewed on the phone, offered and accepted the post, and moved to Boston just prior to Labor Day. During many of the seven years she lived in Boston, she was romantically involved with a marine biologist who lived in Provincetown and worked at the Cape Cod National Seashore. She visited Provincetown almost weekly for years and had no knowledge of her family's connection to the community. Unknowingly she walked past Dr. Thompson's home at 599 Commercial Street countless times. After Clara Thompson died, the home was purchased by the CEO of Abercrombie and Fitch.

The author lived with one of Henry's paintings her entire life, but did not know it. When Silvia died in 2003 she was given a painting that had hung in the house for decades. She remembered the painting since childhood. She thought Silvia said it was painted by her own godfather, but now realizes her mother meant her godfather. It now makes sense that Silvia's godfather would be also her Uncle Henry, nicknamed Sicu by the family. The author never knew his name and as a child showed little interest to get additional information from her mother. The painting is a small oil of a dune shack surrounded by pine trees, shrubs, and beach grasses. It was painted in Provincetown, most likely in the 1930s, and was part of a New York showing in the 1950s after his death. It is believed that Alexander obtained the painting for his daughter Silvia at the time as she spent summers on Cape Cod as a young child.

In 2010, as her family history began to unfold for the author, her cousin Stella (the daughter of Lilla) sent her a book on Henry Major. When she saw the signature on the reproduced paintings in the book, she immediately took the book to compare the signature on the oil painting that now hangs in the parlor. She had been unable to decipher the writing before. It was then that she had an epiphany. The picture the author had known and loved for many years was painted by none other than her great-uncle. The author now knows that she is one of only two family members who have one of Sicu's oil paintings. And to know he walked the same streets she did, forty years earlier, brings her a feeling of continuity and belonging never felt before. And, the picture is of a place she spent nearly every weekend for years. Is that irony or coincidence, neither or both?

Erzsi's daughter Edith would find some success on the Broadway stage as a playwright and actress. She changed her name to Leyla George and died before her mother, in 1945, due to diabetes. The family says she likely wanted to die. A cousin said Leyla knew about the damage that chocolate would bring to her and continued to consume large quantities of chocolate bars. She died in a diabetic coma.

Magdalena Alexander (Revesz)

Magdalena is the third daughter and third child born to Bernard and Regina. Magda was born on September 13, 1885. Like her sisters before her, she was born in Budapest while her father was a professor of philosophy. Like the other children, she was raised in a fairly genteel and proper home, with high expectations, where roles were traditional, yet with opportunities to be exposed to literature and the arts. She studied art in Budapest at the Royal Academy at a time when women did not obtain much formal education and completed her doctorate degree before marriage. Like her older sister Erzsi, she was neither handsome nor beautiful. She was demanding, persistent, formidable, and strived for perfection in herself and wanted that from others as well. She appears to have been rather rigid and unforgiving toward others in the family, a trait shared with others. In her work she was exacting, competent, dedicated, and considered an expert.

In June 1910 Magda married Dr. Geza Revesz, a Jewish Hungarian psychologist whose interest was in industrial psychology and who played a major role in the development of European psychology. Geza and Magda had just one child, Judith, who is one hundred years old and who lives in Malcesine, Italy where her family vacationed for decades in the summer months. Judith was born in 1915 and in 1920 the family left Budapest and moved to the Netherlands where her father worked at the University of Amsterdam. He rarely saw private patients and furthered the field of music psychology. He did, however, agree to see one patient, the first wife of August Eduard von Saher, who would meet his future wife, Lilla, at her uncle's office.

During the years in Holland Magda continued her work in the field of art history and wrote several books. Her daughter Judith describes her as someone who was difficult to please and who had extremely high

Magda Alexander

standards. When Judith, a skilled and talented ceramicist, indicated her desire to study in Budapest, her mother was initially disappointed she was not going to be an academician. She did, then, fully support her daughter's interest in ceramics. Magda, unlike most of the other siblings, never did immigrate to America. Judith says, with some sadness, that "America swallowed up my whole family," when she refers to those who left Europe and, ostensibly, left her behind.

Judith married Henrik Laqueur whose father was Dr. Ernst Laqueur. In 1920 Dr. Laqueur was appointed professor of pharmacology at the University of Amsterdam. It was not until 1932 that Dr. Laqueur would become a Dutch citizen. In 1940, the Netherlands was occupied by German troops. As a result, Laqueur lost his university appointment because of his Jewish ancestry just as Bernard had more than twenty years before. In 1944 Ernst Laqueur was deported to a concentration camp. The end of the war saved his life. This denial of Jewish heritage is mentioned as it parallels the Alexander story. Magda did not raise Judith as a Jew. Neither did Judith raise her two children as Jewish. So we have parents, again, who refuse to accept or deny their Jewish heritage and lineage and as a consequence, part of their self is lost.

Paul Alexander

Paul was born in Budapest in 1896. He was the second son born to his parents, just five years after his older brother, the author's grandfather.

Right to left: Magda Alexander, Dr. Geza Revesz, Judith Revesz and unknown family friends.

He is the fifth of seven children and is said to have been adored by his younger siblings, Borbala and Lilla. During World War I he was a cavalry officer in the Hungarian Army though never did see action in the war. He cut a striking figure in his army uniform, being taller and more slender than the other Broessler/Alexander children. He wore clothes well and can be described as quite handsome. Paul could perhaps best be considered debonair, unlike his older brother who was rather frumpy and whose build resembled Babe Ruth as one of his colleagues, Dr. Leon Saul, said in a tribute written after Alexander's death.

After the war was over, Paul moved to Berlin where his brother, Feri, went earlier to enter the Berlin Psychoanalytic Institute as its first student. Their younger sister, Lilla, had also moved to Berlin, as a teenager, to further her dreams to become a screen star. She had been taken under the wing of a successful movie producer at only sixteen. Paul, known as Pali in the family, was working at a Czech bank in Berlin, the only routine position he ever held, and there met his future wife, Irina Constantinova. Covi, as nicknamed by Pali, was working as a foreign correspondent in the same bank. Covi, like Feri's wife, was raised in a convent school. She, like Feri's wife, was extremely beautiful. She was considered brilliant at the bank, and had good career prospects for the future. But they soon married, and later moved to Budapest to live with his father, his sister Borka and her husband, and their baby boy, Alfred Rényi. The move back to Budapest meant that Paul was unable to complete his doctorate. Covi was brilliant in many ways; she was multilingual, and spoke Czech, German, Hungarian, and English, and was very well read. Her landscaping and gardening abilities were highly respected—garden clubs in England always wanted to tour her garden. She was especially known for her cooking, although she had had no experience in this prior to her marriage. Covi and Paul had two daughters born to them in Budapest before moving away to England.

Paul began to specialize in developing high vacuum technology, and developed the diffusion pump. A Dutch company had become interested, and so the family, including the young daughters, Catherine and Vera, moved to Holland. In 1935 his work was noticed by a Belgian company, so, once again, the family moved, now to Brussels. In 1936 he made an even better agreement with Pilkington Brothers, a British glass manufacturer in St. Helens, Lancashire. Paul and Covi rented a Victorian house in Huyton, a village just three miles from St. Helens and about ten miles from Liverpool. In 1940,

Paul Alexander

Paul made an agreement with the gold foil beating firm of George M. Whiley, located in London. This necessitated another move, to be closer to work, and the family settled in the small town of Berkhamsted in Hertfordshire. Here they spent the war years. Paul made highly significant improvements in the ability to produce ultra-high vacuums and, based on this, invented the technique for evaporating metals in high vacuum chambers and depositing them in single-molecular layers on materials. Particularly relevant was the ability to produce very thin metallic coatings on a then-new material, Mylar. Part of his research during those years was done at the Cavendish Laboratories at Cambridge University, and part was done in London. He had been fortunate during his whole career to retain all the patents for himself, and in 1950 he decided to move to the United States to initiate the manufacture of coated Mylar himself. By this time his sister Borka was dead and the rest of his siblings, except for Magda, had adopted America as their home. He had already set up a company in England to assist with his new endeavors.

The family, now with a son Robin born in 1943, moved to America and settled in Princeton, New Jersey, and Pali established a pilot plant in nearby Hightstown. This process could have been worth a fortune, but unfortunately he sold out to the Minnesota Mining and Manufacturing Company, just in time for them to profit from the developing market for radar reflectors and for the space program in general.

Paul's daughter Vera has many happy memories of times spent with her father's siblings and knew them all, but was too young to remember Borka. Covi always adored Borka. Erzsi came from America to join Pali and his family for a postwar vacation in Switzerland. The family also went to the Netherlands after the war to visit Magda and Geza in Amsterdam and Vera saw Magda again in 1965. Vera knew Lilla well and was the only close family member who came to visit her in the hospital when she was dying. Vera became good friends with Mark Riwkin, Lilla's second husband, one summer during a joint vacation on Cape Cod. This summer followed Vera's first year of college in Madison at the University of Wisconsin. It certainly appears that Paul and his children continued the tradition set by Bernard and Regina of vacationing with family and keeping close family ties.

Paul died of lung cancer in 1959 and Covi of a stroke in 1974. Their daughter Catherine studied astrophysics. Their daughter Vera became a world-famous oceanographer and would be the first woman to be granted a doctorate from the University of Alaska. Their son Robin would obtain his doctorate in accounting and inherited his mother's aptitude and love of cooking.

Although Paul, along with his older brother, warned their younger sister Lilla about not telling the family secret of their Jewish heritage, Paul did not consider himself Jewish and neither do any of his descendants.

Borbala Alexander (Renyi)

Borbala, or Barbara, is the sixth of seven children born to her parents. She was born in Budapest on July 27, 1899. She was a keen observer of

Regina Broessler Alexander and Paul Alexander in Budapest.

people and became interested in photography at an early age. Many of her photos, taken of her brother's children, Catherine and Vera, when they moved in with her, are still in the family. Borbala, oddly enough, was never mentioned by Alexander to the family as one of his siblings. Alexander's firstborn daughter, Silvia, never mentioned her name as she did not know of her existence. When a friend of the author located her name on the internet, it had never been heard before. Questions arose. How could the life of one whole person be kept a secret when other names were known? Memorial writings about Alexander, written by his colleagues and fellow analysts after his death, speak of how Paul and Borka, her nickname, adored their older brother, Feri. The author now wonders if this was fiction and represents another story to reflect positively back to Alexander and his own father. It is true, however, that Lilla and Borka adored their older brother Paul. It is doubtful that Borka, near the end of her life, adored Alexander who appears to have almost abandoned her after the war when she needed help badly. Or, to be fair, perhaps she asked only for minimal help from him, fearing reprisal by the then communist regimen.

Borka met her husband Artur, a mechanical engineer and linguist, in Budapest when he called on her during Easter 1920 to set up a photography session. Artur's father was born in Germany and carried the name Rosenthal. He changed his name to Renyi and eventually settled in Hungary. He owned a walking cane company and made his fortune in Hungary.

The day after meeting Borka, Artur proposed marriage and she accepted. They soon travelled to Vienna and then to Ebenhausen, a

Borka Alexander

town in Bavaria where Borka's mother was recuperating from a series of strokes. Borka wanted to get her father's approval in order to marry Artur. The couple married in Budapest on May 4, 1920. Artur was devoted to Borka and when she died at a young age, in her forties, because of a stroke in 1946, he was devastated. He wrote freely and openly about his feelings in his diary, which has been passed down to his great granddaughter Nauszika, a school psychologist living in Budapest, who has shared many passages with the author.

Borka and Artur had one child, Alfred, who was born in 1921 in the same month as Alexander's firstborn. In old family photographs, Borka and Artur stroll with a young Alfred, perhaps close to Margaret's Island in Budapest. Others depict Alfred studying or playing with an erector set. Alfred was nicknamed Buba, Hungarian for baby, and his close friends called him this throughout his short life. Borka took photos of Alfred holding a young Vera or Catherine. Alfred is always smiling and looks happy in the photographs. Like the generation of Alexander children before him, Alfred's education at the gymnasium was mostly literary instead of scientific. Alfred is said to have had a love of literature and Greek philosophy, no doubt an influence of his mother's from her father, Bernard. His interest in astronomy and physics led him to mathematics. At the time he was ready to enter university in 1939 anti-Semitism was so strong in Hungary that college was not available to him. This despite the fact he graduated from the gymnasium at the top of his class. And despite the fact his family, neither his parents, nor his grandparents before him, practised the Jewish faith or its customs.

Artur Renyi, his wife Borbala and their son Alfred in the early 1930s.

Buba's story is one of extreme bravery in the face of danger that one can only pretend to understand. Instead of attending university right after the gymnasium, he entered the workforce as a laborer and worked for a short while in a shipping company. He was eventually able to enrol in the University of Budapest in late 1940 where he studied numbers theory. He graduated in 1944 and was then forced into a fascist labor camp from which he was somehow able to escape. For a period of six months or more he lived with false papers before World War II ended. His parents were placed in a Budapest ghetto, most likely in preparation for transport to Auschwitz. Showing heroism to be admired, Alfred donned a Hungarian officer's uniform, walked into the ghetto with authority and grace, and freed his parents. Had it not been for his keeping calm under extreme conditions, his parents would have no doubt been two of the 600,000 Hungarian Jews who were murdered by the Nazis.

Alfred later completed his doctorate from the University of Szeged and worked diligently until his early death in 1970 at the age of forty-eight. He and his wife, Kaitlin Scholhof, also a mathematician of considerable prestige, had one child, a daughter, Zsuzsi. Zsuzsi lives in Budapest and has one daughter, Nauszika.

Paul Turán (1970) writes of Rényi, though this could have been written about Alexander … as they both were energetic and full of life: *Rényi's zest for life was by no means exhausted in his many-sided intellectual activities and involvement in public affairs. He was fond of rowing and swimming in the Danube in summer and of skiing in winter. With his wife and daughter Zsuzsi he frequented concerts and theatres; at the parties they gave in their home, Rényi entertained his friends with witty anecdotes and with playing the piano. Those entering his study were welcomed by bookshelves jammed to the ceiling. The books, manuscripts and notes scattered on his desk made the visitor feel that he had entered the scene of creative, productive activity, an activity that Alfred Rényi carried on unabated to the last day of his life.*

David Kendall (1976) writes as well: … *a pure mathematician of massive achievements and towering stature in the classical fields of number theory and analysis. Rényi possessed also an inquisitive and dogged interest in all the phenomena of the world about him, and in all the scholarly activities of his colleagues, whether scientific or humane, and this unique combination of powers and interests enabled him to build up a research institute in which the criterion for acceptability of a subject for investigation was "does there exist at least one mathematician with a genuine interest in this topic"? Once accepted as appropriate, however, the topic would be pursued in a thoroughly professional way; the argument would be followed wherever it led, and buttressed by whatever mathematical means seemed appropriate, however exotic or sophisticated.*

It was during these late war years that Borka wrote to her older brother Alexander in America, asking for assistance. She and her family lost everything during the war. The apartment at 24 Belgrade Street, that had been her home for more than thirty years, was taken from her. Artur lost his job. At the same time, Alexander carved for himself a successful niche in Chicago. He had academic and material success. He was considered the highest achiever of all the Alexander children and his was often the yardstick against which others' success, or lack thereof, was measured. Alexander, according to Artur's diaries, sent his sister $40 on two separate occasions and some food. It is not known why he sent this meager contribution. It is unknown if this is what she asked of him at the time. He certainly had the resources as it was at the same time he offered a $50,000 bribe to his granddaughter's father and was rumored to be charging in excess of $100 an hour for psychoanalysis. Artur's diaries, though eloquent, insightful, and poignant, do not provide this answer.

After Borka died in 1946 there was no further contact between the Rényis and Alexander. Artur was lost without his wife and became somewhat depressed. Artur died just four years after Borka in 1950 and by that time, Alfred was a world-famous mathematician, had travelled to America many times, and had met many of his cousins. Alfred considered himself Jewish.

It most certainly seems that Borka and her son Alfred lived up to the high expectations of Bernard Alexander. From all stories from cousins, Borka adored her father and was very family minded. She also took in Paul and his wife Covi in the early days of their marriage. And yet, again, why had some not heard her name? Is it because her family was identified as Hungarian Jews and the Alexanders did everything to distance themselves from Jews? The extent of their bravery and courage would not be known until decades later when Artur's diary was made known to the rest of the Alexander family.

Lillian Alexander (von Saher, Riwkin)

Lillian Theodora was Bernard and Regina Alexander's seventh and last child. Little Lilla, as she later called herself, worshiped her father but had scant recollection of her mother during her childhood, and who died when she was twenty years old. Lilla was raised by her older sister Erzsi as their mother began to have health problems when Lilla was young. Lilla remembered many important people, from Hungary and elsewhere, who came to visit the family. Her childhood was idyllic with summer trips to a farm in the country. Her only childhood tragedy was the slaughter of her favorite pig. She also remembered that the family was poor and that she had only hand-me-down clothing and toys but never a new dress or doll. Later when she married Lilla bought herself seventy dolls. This recollection, passed on to her daughter Stella, appears to be in direct contrast with memories from her siblings as well as from academic writings that describe the household as "opulent and upper middle class intelligentsia." Lilla was described by a cousin, Eva Broessler Weissman, as a fibber, and one who liked to embellish the truth. This trait of telling lies and fabricating more interesting versions of their lives is seen in most of the family members.

In 1918, at the age of sixteen, Lillian, still almost a child, left Budapest, and joined the famed Hungarian director, Arzen de Cserepy, who promised her fame as an actress. He would direct her in several films. Lilla, as she would then be known, also acted in stage productions in both France and Germany. At that time her older brother Feri was living in Berlin with his wife Anita and studying at the Berlin Psychoanalytic Institute. Lilla was dramatic and mesmerizing when acting but also in her private life. Lilla's magnetic personality and presence made her the focus of any party where she made spectacular and dramatic entrances. She was beautiful and oozed with the Alexander charm. She acted in films opposite and directed by famed French film director/actor Jean Renoir. In Paris, on the theatre stage, she starred as Cleopatra. It looked like her film and theatre career was forging ahead. For publicity, the studio would occasionally bring her an exotic cat (once a black puma to match her raven hair) to walk on the Unter den Linden boulevard in Berlin or on the Avenue des Champs-Élysées in Paris. Lilla had a life-long passion for cats and was thrilled to be the center of attention with her "film studio" cat. During her film and stage career Lilla met many of Europe's most famous film performers and directors, including French author Sidonie-Gabrielle Colette who shared her love of cats. But, like her older sister who hoped for fame as an opera singer and then as a coach to the movie stars in Hollywood, and her brother who hoped for success as a physicist, true success would evade her.

Lilla Alexander

In 1928, while visiting her sister Magda in Amsterdam, Lilla met and fell in love with an international corporate attorney, August Edward Dimitri von Saher, a married Dutchman with three young children. Mr. von Saher's corporate clients included the Holland America Line, Royal Dutch Shell, and a number of other large global corporations. Soon after they met, Edward von Saher, as he was known, head over heels in love, divorced his wife and married Lilla, who gave up her acting career in favor of motherhood. Their first child, Tibor Alexander von Saher, was born in 1929 while Lilla and her husband were enjoying the third act of *The Three Musketeers* at a theatre in Berlin. They dashed to a nearby hospital. In 1936, a daughter, Stella Maria Regina von Saher, was born. The family thrived, entertained lavishly, and travelled widely throughout Europe. The whole family, together with their two Siamese cats, spent part of each summer in Cap d'Antibes in the South of France for summer vacations where they met and socialized with Joseph and Rose Kennedy.

Edward von Saher was the premier collector of works by Pablo Picasso in the Netherlands. He also collected works by Juan Gris, Fernand Leger, Braque, and other soon-to-be famous artists. Picasso's "Portrait of Clovis Sagot," 1909, hung above the fireplace.

A dark cloud was looming over Europe as Hitler came into power and Edward felt it was too dangerous to remain in Europe with his secretly Jewish wife and their two children. The family sailed on the *SS Rex* to Canada and finally settled in New York City at an architecturally stunning full-floor residence on Fifth Avenue overlooking Central Park, the Reservoir, the city skyline and, later, the Guggenheim Museum. Edward used the enormous front room as his law library office and employed two full time secretaries whose offices were at the back of the large apartment.

The family car also came to New York, a 1937 Packard V12 convertible that had been used by Queen Wilhelmina and her family upon their return to the Netherlands after the WWII armistice. One special moment was being introduced to the country's beloved queen at the royal palace in 1939. British Prime Minister Churchill used it for his post-WWII visit to the Netherlands on May 13, 1946.

During the war years, safe in the United States, Lilla worked for the Red Cross, drove an ambulance, and did translations of correspondence in five languages at the United States Census Bureau in New York. She also wrote her first novel, *The Echo*, about a woman who goes to a psychiatrist, a highly unusual topic for 1947. Lilla's older brother, Alexander, was already well known as the founder of the Chicago Psychoanalytic Institute.

Nearing the end of World War II, Edward wrote a landmark and definitive law brief regarding the disposal of an enemy ship, the *Janko*, captured at the end of WWII in Christianstaad, Curacao, a Dutch territory then under German rule. Lilla accompanied her husband to Curacao and began to write her second published novel, *Macamba*, about a love affair between a West Indian man and a white woman—another very daring and unusual topic. She wrote three published books, with *Exotic Cookery* being the last one. Still ravishingly beautiful and with a great sense of allure, she went on book tours around the United States and willingly autographed copies of her works. Her heavy Hungarian accent added to her mystique. Lilla became friends with Charles Revson, the founder of Revlon Salons, and she always dressed in beautiful and expensive fashionable clothing. Her hats were designed especially for her by Jacques Fath.

Lilla had always looked younger than her years and was vibrant and full of life and now was married to an aging husband. In 1948, Lilla met Matisyahu (Mark) Alexandrovich Riwkin, a dark brooding Russian man at a party. Riwkin was born in Surazh, Belarus but grew up in Sweden. It was the first time that Lilla had been unfaithful to her husband. Mark was a man with no single profession. He was an "ideas man" and saw connections others did not see. He took a sales pitch about a process invented by Lilla's brother, Paul, a physicist, to a major American company (Continental Can) and received over $900,000 for his idea. When he needed money, Mark searched for a new endeavor. One such venture was importing the Modern Art Catalogue Raisonné by Skira, richly illustrated dossiers on the works of various artists such as Paul Gauguin, Le Corbusier, and others.

Lilla's husband, Edward, was heartbroken when Lilla left him and married Mark Riwkin. He felt his advancing age, became deeply depressed, and suffered a serious heart attack. His business associates noticed his despair and, before long, he was befriended and consoled by an acquaintance from the Dutch community in New York City. Desire von Halban was a wealthy widow with a young son, Edo. Once Edward and Lilla's divorce was final, the couple married and Edward tried to forge a new life. He was always deeply wounded by Lilla's departure. This new marriage was one of mutual need and the couple tried to make it work.

Lilla meanwhile was travelling with her new husband and daughter and also trying to write. She had met Tennessee Williams, Gore Vidal, Edward Albee, Jerzy Kosinski, James Baldwin, and other known writers. In this circle of writer and theatre friends Mark, Lilla, and her daughter, Stella, were known as the Count, the Duchess and the Princess. Lilla wrote several plays but only one, *Three Days with Aria*, was published (translated into German) but was never brought to the stage, a great disappointment. Mark wanted to wander from country to country visiting friends while Lilla wanted to return to New York—and she did so alone.

In New York, Lilla continued to write. However, she was diagnosed with a virulent form of breast cancer. Lilla was in denial as her cancer spread, creating the illusion she had been delivered of a baby. She sent relatives and friends photographs of herself depicted as pregnant and then actually holding a baby named Alyosha in her arms, all at her very advanced age. She had no more money left from her settlement with Edward, and Mark had committed suicide. She was desperate and destitute. Lilla died in 1969 at the age of sixty-seven in New York's Beth Israel Hospital under the generous and kind care of a cousin, Eva Broessler Weissman, whose husband, Oscar, was the hospital administrator. Lilla was buried in a charity grave in a Jewish cemetery on Long Island. She never admitted to her children or friends that she was Jewish. Lilla's death was a sad ending to a life started in Budapest that held so much promise for the beautiful and talented girl who became a movie and stage star, married a very wealthy man who loved her, had two healthy children, and then married a Belarus adventurer who gave her many exciting years of travel and new experiences. She is the only Alexander sibling the author met. She came to California for Alexander's funeral in the spring of 1964.

Lies through the decades

It may be that the lies told by the Alexanders, to deny their Jewish heritage, may have at their nucleus always the same motivation: To belong; to be accepted; to be liked; and to protect. Jews have been hated and despised throughout their entire history. Bernard Alexander was a distinguished scholar and a celebrated intellect. He had been provided an opportunity to obtain an excellent education and to gain success and a following among upper middle class intelligentsia. He had seemingly been accepted by the Christian society of Budapest, and across most of Europe, but most likely always feared the possibility that those who accepted him might eventually turn on him. When that happened, in the days after World War I, and the incident was witnessed by the entire Alexander family, it had cataclysmic for all of them. It was as if the family learned, at that time, that complete and full acceptance would be denied to them and any other Jew as well. What had begun for Bernard as a simple going along with an existing custom, denying Jewish heritage in order to be accepted and belong to the university community, took on more serious connotations.

To deny one's heritage is to tell the most basic of lies. To erase and deny heritage is to eliminate self-knowledge. To perfect one's public self often means that a complete and deliberate obfuscation of family roots occurs and sometimes it is necessary to change family history. When this is allowed to happen, family is excluded from future generations. Hiding Jewish heritage and making up history was rampant as a tool to survive in the Alexander household. This resulted in the generations being denied knowledge of family and history as lies and secrets were perpetuated for decades and were begun, apparently, by Bernard Alexander. It would not be until 2009, when the author began to unravel family secrets and learn of relatives kept from her, that the family would again come together for the first time in decades.

This reliance on lies, and the need to belong and be seen as perfect, led to Alexander's behavior intended to keep separate his public and private self. He insulated and protected himself from his feelings and was slow to express his feelings to others. He was very uncomfortable when others attempted to share their feelings with him. This is why his children often said he did not seem to care about them or their achievements. He most certainly did care; he did not know how to express it. When his youngest daughter obtained her doctorate, he shook her hand. She had hoped for a warm embrace. Affection was rarely expressed in the household, either between Alexander and his wife or from either parent to the children. In the children's adult years, there would be long periods of estrangement from each other and from their mother.

In the Alexander family, the ravages of nonacceptance, fear, and paranoia continue to plague some in the current generations. In order to protect itself against such assaults, the Alexander family closed ranks long ago, parenthetically, and became non-Jewish. Even after the disclosure and discovery of Jewish connections, most ignored the information and continued to live lives as if nothing important had been learned. The rage felt at what occurred during the Holocaust is felt by those who were then not alive and seems only to be felt in a superficial, intellectual manner as Jewishness is still not accepted. Only one of the Alexander sibling's descendants has embraced the idea of being Jewish. The author, learning of her Jewish heritage in 2008, is absorbing its meaning as well as accepting her family's lies and secrets.

Whatever the reason was, truth telling was not adopted as the norm by the Alexanders when the need to protect oneself was felt. The author considers this scheme, to deny heritage and to lie about history, and to eliminate family and a father from a young child's life, to be most difficult to understand. It is certainly not what one would expect from Franz Alexander. As in the childhood story about the emperor's new clothes, it is clear that Alexander, too, had feet of clay and was capable of major missteps when forced to make important decisions regarding family. Like the emperor, he often operated in the world of "as if." Like many said after his death, few knew him, really knew him.

CHAPTER FIVE

Berlin: setting the stage for Chicago (with a brief stopover in Boston)

Post-war adjustment came slowly to Alexander. During his time in Berlin he wrote, "I saw the world of my youth rapidly disintegrate and standards and ideals that had become second nature to me vanish … Everyone expected the worst, was worried, strained, and concerned about himself, and with his uncertain future, and with the pressing and practical concerns about the present." Like most at the time who had experienced the Great War, Alexander was demoralized, and he was demoralized when he left Budapest and came to Berlin. It was especially difficult for him to accept the effects of war on Hungary and the breakup of the Austro-Hungarian Empire as well as the effects of war on his family.

Berlin in the early 1920s was often violent and unpredictable. Alexander called it "stimulating chaos" (Alexander & Eissler, 1954) though it was not altogether a comfortable time for him. Alexander found Berlin to be quite different from his opulent native Budapest. Berlin was coarser, with an edge to it.

The end of World War I and the signing of the Armistice caused Germany great humiliation. Germany thought it had been winning the war. Hitler later skillfully used propaganda to inform the German people of this, as if it were true, and manipulated them. When the

Armistice was signed, Germany thought it was a truce; the rest of the world considered it surrender. Germans believed that the conditions of reparation imposed on them were unusually harsh. Germany considered herself grievously injured and thought of herself as a victim. In contrast to the prosperity seen in other European cities after World War I, Berlin was ravaged by turmoil and financial chaos and the mark became worthless. It was a harsh change from the prewar days of prosperity as Germany entered the years under the Weimar Republic prior to the Third Reich. Throughout most of the fifteen years the Weimar Republic existed, Alexander lived and worked in Berlin.

One of the consequences of most wars, when young men leave their homes and families, is the demand that jobs vacated be filled by women. During World War I women drove taxis, worked on the engines of cars, labored in factories and in construction; in effect, took on the tasks left fallow when men go to war. When the war was over, and the men returned, often broken and unwell, the women were free to attend university and pursue their own interests. In the years between 1920 and 1923, the mark continued to fall as Germany had enormous reparations to pay. Money was worthless and the jobs held by women during the war were now vacant as unemployment rose higher and higher with each year. People were depressed and without hope.

Against this backdrop began the Berlin Psychoanalytic Institute. Dr. Max Eitingon came to Vienna from Zurich to attend a meeting of the Vienna Psychoanalytic Society on January 23, 1907. The society, originally named the Wednesday Psychological Society, was the small group of psychoanalysts who started to meet in Freud's apartment in 1902. By 1908 the group had changed its name and was regarded as the authority on psychoanalysis. In addition to attending these meetings, Eitingon also had come to Vienna to gain access to Freud. He sought Freud's expertise regarding a difficult patient in Burghölzli at the recommendation of Bleuler. Eitingon was interested to learn how psychoanalysis could benefit a psychiatrist, and stayed on, taking long walks with Freud. Those walks, lasting no more than five weeks, were one of Freud's early psychoanalyses. Eitingon became the first foreigner to study psychoanalysis at the source, with Freud, in Vienna. Freud often would say that Eitingon was the first to come and spend time with the lonely man.

Eitingon joined the Secret Committee as Freud's health began to deteriorate in the days after World War I. The committee was a group of six other psychoanalysts who formed an alliance in order to ensure that psychoanalysis remained pure and adhered to Freud's theories. The group was to "to maintain the faith and to search out deviance" according to Phyllis Grosskurth in *The Secret Ring: Freud's Inner Circle and the Politics of Psychoanalysis* (Grosskurth, 1991, pp. 20–21). The group's members included Otto Rank, Hanns Sachs, Karl Abraham, Ernest Jones, Max Eitingon, and Sandor Ferenczi. This committee, formed between 1912 and 1913, fell apart in 1927. There are differing views as to why it broke up, including self-destruction and the accomplishment of its goal: to spread and nurture psychoanalysis around the globe.

Eitingon was a striking man with a slightly balding head and wire-rimmed glasses. He looked intellectual and was prepared to take on the task of establishing an institute singlehandedly. He came from an extremely wealthy family and his father was a fur trader and had come from Russia to settle in Germany. Eitingon was the only psychoanalyst at the time to have financial means of his own. He used his own financial resources to set up the institute. Eitingon would eventually provide the institute with the funds to support most of the treatment provided to its poor patients as less than ten percent could pay for their own treatment. Eitingon founded the Berlin Psychoanalytic Institute with Karl Abraham, and enlisted Freud's favorite son Ernst to design the clinic and do the interior décor as well.

Karl Abraham was introduced to psychoanalysis by Carl Jung while studying medicine in Switzerland with Paul Eugen Bleuler. After Abraham met Freud in 1907, the two remained close friends throughout their lives and Freud described Abraham as his best pupil ever. After he completed his medical studies in Switzerland, Abraham returned to Berlin and founded the Berlin Psychoanalytical Society in 1910. Abraham collaborated with Freud on what was then called manic-depressive illness; Freud published "Mourning and Melancholia" in 1917. Abraham was considered to be a mentor to Alexander and to his nemesis, Karen Horney, when they were both at the Berlin Institute.

The Berlin Institute's goals were to train analysts as well as provide treatment to all those suffering with neuroses including the indigent patients in Berlin. A third goal was to refine techniques and knowledge with research. These goals may have appeared lofty and idealistic at the time, and most important, the goals were to be supported and backed up by Freud's theories of psychoanalysis. It is essential to remember that Freud was known primarily as a researcher and not a clinician. He

was interested in seeking knowledge for its own sake. In that, Freud
was like the professor father, Bernard Alexander, who believed that the
pursuit of knowledge, for its own sake, was the reward. Alexander says
in his semi-autobiographic work, *The Western Mind in Transition*, that
the generation of his father and his intellectual colleagues, as well as his
own, was one that encouraged and appreciated intellectual and artistic
accomplishments as well as generating creativity. Those ideals were
held in the highest esteem by both Alexander and his father before him
and would influence psychoanalysis as well.

It was Eitingon who took Freud's concepts and designed a true
model for the training of psychoanalysts; Alexander would take that
model to Chicago when he founded the second American institute in
1932; and elements of that model are still used today. It was the work
in Berlin that reinforced for Alexander the importance of research as
the foundation for policies and procedures, and ultimately, the foundation for the Chicago Institute. Alexander then first began to consider
the importance of working with community partners, lay boards, and
suggested the validity of training lay analysts as he had the personal
experience of being analysed by a nonmedical analyst, Hanns Sachs.
This dedication to and reliance on research and the need to embrace
new ideas was a different practice than seeking knowledge for its own
sake and a true deviation from the ideals of his professor father and
well as Professor Freud.

In the autumn of 1920 Alexander went to Berlin where he was
accepted as the first student at the Berlin Psychoanalytic Institute.
After a year or more of planning, meetings, and discussions, the Berlin
Institute officially opened its doors on February 14, 1920. Staff of the
Poliklinik included Karen Horney, Hans Liebermann, Felix Boehm,
Carl Müller-Braunschweig, and Alexander's future analyst, Hanns
Sachs. Alexander had already met Freud when he began his studies in
Berlin. By making the decision to go to Berlin to study psychoanalysis, he gave up all plans for an illustrious academic career in formal
psychiatry. He had been won over by the clinical observational methods
of psychoanalysis. He did not realize it at the time, but psychoanalysis
would also prove to be of benefit personally as it allowed him to work
through his issues of insecurity and being a disappointment to his
father. At the time of his studies, he felt alone and isolated. He was
living away from his family, his wife was pregnant, and he felt little
professional support.

Being in Berlin offered Alexander an opportunity to return to the journey he left behind when drafted into the Hungarian Army as World War I began. This would be the life to which he would ultimately and wholeheartedly devote himself. Berlin represented a return to the philosophical pursuits of knowledge which had been a strong tradition in the family as well as an opportunity to try new ideas. As Alexander concentrated on his pursuit of psychoanalysis, he was immune to the development of politics around him during the days of the Weimar Republic. Most of those present at the institute were naïve regarding German politics after World War I. He admits to living in an ivory tower and being consumed with only thoughts of work during his interview with Kurt Eissler in 1954. By joining the ranks of other psychoanalysts, who were kept outside the traditional medical community, he was, then, part of a marginal group without the usual prestige or respect. Analysts at the time became members of the International Psycho-Analytical Association under the leadership of Freud. The local societies that had sprung up all over Europe provided a safe haven and the group started to become more and more insular and isolated. The members were bound together in a new field seen by others as outsiders. Everyone knew each other personally regardless of where they practised. Alexander and the others had no doubt that psychoanalysis would take hold and change the face of psychiatric treatment and the social sciences, but others in the medical community were not so optimistic. They, slow to jump on board, would be a thorn in Alexander's side for quite some time. When he was able to see the big picture, and others could not, he could be impatient. Soon, however, this initial lack of respect would turn to admiration as he continued his work in Berlin in the newly emerging science of psychoanalysis.

Psychoanalysis had yet to be completely accepted by the medical professionals. Although psychoanalysis was spreading and societies were springing up in America and throughout Europe, it was still not thought of as scientific and was poorly understood. Psychoanalytic journals were becoming prolific and the European societies, quiet during the Great War, were again meeting and flourishing, but little was known or accepted in the purely scientific world of psychiatry. This climate fostered what was labelled as analytic infighting by Alexander. This infighting among colleagues would challenge him periodically throughout his career, in different countries, whenever new ideas were proposed. His isolation did not, however, prevent him from totally immersing himself in his studies. He was someone who did not start a project without a total commitment.

At that time, training for analysts did not mean a regular protocol, curriculum, or standards in the manner we understand today. There was no such thing as scope of practice. The institute provided lectures and opportunities for the training analysts to see patients and integrate theoretical knowledge with actual cases. By 1922 a formal training program was agreed upon that allowed a student to enter and complete psychoanalytic training in eighteen months. As now, in order to graduate as a psychoanalyst, one had to undergo a personal analysis. The challenge, though, was how to define what constituted a personal analysis and what form and style it should take. Many argued that the candidates were essentially healthy individuals, what we now call the worried well, and the analysis should be educational and not therapeutic. At the time everything was pretty much made up "on the fly." Whoever presented to the institute and asked to be trained was accepted. It was an informal system with few rules. Everyone knew each other and was on friendly terms. The issue of how to bring together the clinical theory with practical experience challenged the staff for quite a while. This same challenge presents itself today in schools everywhere as clinicians and theoreticians attempt to merge these essential divergent elements. The work to establish a proper training protocol for the institute would consume its staff for years, well into 1924. Eventually a training committee was formed and a formal curriculum was adopted in 1925. Though Alexander delighted in saying he was the first student of the Berlin Institute, there was no real program at the time. Technically, however, he was correct with his statement.

Alexander entered into his analysis with Hanns Sachs soon after coming to the institute. Sachs had been appointed the first training analyst at the Berlin Institute despite his not being a psychiatrist. Sachs's background was legal and he had been a practising lawyer when he first met and began to follow Freud. Sachs had nevertheless been accepted as part of Freud's inner circle in Vienna and he became a member of the Secret Committee. Alexander's analysis with Sachs was, however, by no means a traditional one. He and Sachs took walks and discussed various issues in a rather informal manner. Instead of meeting almost daily for a year or more, in an office and on a couch, this so-called analysis lasted about three months. At that time Alexander told Sachs about an oedipal dream. Sachs told him he was cured and the analysis ended.

It is possible that the genesis of Alexander's belief that analysis did not have to be long in order to be successful may have formed as a result of his short analysis with Sachs.

Alexander and his Italian bride were married again in February 1921, this time in a civil ceremony, presumably because post-World War I Germany did not recognize church weddings. This was a common policy in many European countries at the time. Alexander could hardly pay his living expenses and was given a small salary by the institute to help pay for his family which now included a daughter, Silvia, born in March of 1921. Silvia was the image of her mother and did not have any of the physical characteristics of the Broessler/Alexander clan. She was pretty, petite, blonde, and blue-eyed, just like her mother Annie. She was the perfect daughter for Alexander. When Silvia, as an adult in her seventh decade, learned that her parents were married just a month before her birth, she was horrified to consider hers may have been an illegitimate birth. In actuality this civil ceremony was more than two years after their church ceremony in Italy. This seemingly insignificant fact underscores how personal matters were not discussed at home. Silvia knew little of how her parents met, or that they had married either during the final days of the First World War or immediately after. She assumed, as she feared everyone else would as well, that her parents married "just in time" to legitimize her birth.

In the fall of 1921 Alexander was a full-fledged analyst after completing his studies at the institute. He began to work as the assistant to the director. Other staff members at the time included, in addition to Alexander and Sachs, Sandor Rado, Otto Fenichel, Siegfried Bernfeld, Karen Horney, and Felix Boehm. These illustrious pioneers attracted many students, some from as far away as America, and in the next years additional training institutes were established in Vienna, London, and the Netherlands by other leading pioneer analysts of the time, among them Helene Deutsch and Ernest Jones.

During those early times in Berlin, before Alexander established himself and began to become a financial success as well, his wife Annie supported the family and wrote subtitles for the German motion picture industry and also found additional work as a translator. It was not uncommon for women to support the household during these early days of the Weimar Republic. Money was scarce and Alexander often begged relatives for money and loans. He also sold stamps from his collection or furniture in order to help support the family. He would often later buy back the furniture. Though they were eking out a meager existence at this time, Alexander and his wife were happy and they each prospered in their own right. They were very social and entertained frequently, and had many friends. They lived in the section of Berlin that was close to the Opera House located on Unter den Linden. This section of Berlin would be destroyed by bombs during World War II and become part of what became known as East Berlin during the dark days of communism. Alexander spent his days at the institute. He also had an office at Düsseldorferstrasse 77. He would change the location of his office three more times for reasons that are unknown. It may be that as his financial resources improved, so did his need for a nicer office.

Alexander's mother, Regina Broessler Alexander, died in 1922 after a series of strokes. She had been unwell for several years and went to Switzerland sometime in 1919 for medical treatment, accompanied by her husband. She and her husband then travelled to Ebenhausen, Germany where she entered a nursing home. Bernard remained in Germany with his wife until her death. She was buried in Germany though there is a grave marker in the Jewish Kozma Street cemetery in Budapest. Bernard Alexander returned to live in his former home on Belgrade Street, number 24, overlooking the Elizabeth Bridge and the Danube, in a corner apartment with his daughter, Borbala, and her husband Artur. The building was constructed before the war and built in the art deco style. Borka and her husband had one child, Alfred (Buba) who was born in March 1921 just a week after Silvia.

By the mid-1920s, Berlin was once again a city of excitement and hope. The crushing inflation had ended and the economy became stable again. The cafés were open all night where patrons danced till dawn. Artists, politicians, and musicians sought to escape the reality around them in the many nightclubs. The Berlin cafés were different from those in prewar Budapest. Where Budapest café society was intellectual, Berlin's scene was gay, superficial, and decadent. As Berlin became the new center of intellectual and artistic rebirth in those early days after World War I, so too did it experience the undercurrent of social unrest. Old mores were being challenged and a new liberalism in art, sexuality, film, and literature was emerging. In 1925 Germany elected former field marshal Paul von Hindenburg as her second president, and people were again feeling hopeful and enthusiastic about the future. Women, who had joined the workforce during the war and afterwards, were now turning to other pursuits. The newly elected president of the

Weimar Republic promised good times for all and wanted to lead the government in a more conservative direction. The cabaret scene and spirit of intellectualism would remain vibrant for years as Germany partied once again. This merriment would continue until the next catastrophe hit Germany, the renewed popularity of Hitler, the emergence of the Nazi party, and the events leading to World War II in Europe.

Life in Berlin became settled for the Alexander family in the years after 1925. As Alexander's professional success continued, his wife eventually returned to her artistic pursuits long since abandoned during the war years. She began to seek proper instruction and her instructors, in the cities of Paris, Vienna, and Padua, where she travelled, were generally irritating to her high-strung sensibilities. She soon met Arthur Segal, a Romanian painter who studied in Berlin, and began to take lessons, and she settled down. He was instrumental in her decision to submit a painting for consideration at an important exhibition. In 1926 a second daughter, Francesca, was born. Anna Freud would stand in as her godmother at baptism and Francesca would soon be known by the nickname Kiki. Kiki resembled the Broessler side of the family; she was chubby with dark hair and eyes. Her parents had hoped for a boy and through her growing-up years, she would try to be the boy her father wanted.

In 1927, a year after Kiki was born, Alexander's wife entered a nationwide contest with a painting named "Convent Room." To her surprise, she was awarded first prize by Max Lieberman, an important German impressionist, considered to be the most important German painter at the time. Mr. Lieberman had been totally unaware of Annie when he selected his prize winner. There were more than 300 entries to the contest and Mr. Lieberman assumed the artist was a man. She always signed her work with initials only and when he announced the winner, he began with, "Herr …"

When Annie Alexander came forward to accept the honor, Mr. Lieberman saw an attractive blonde and blue-eyed Italian woman, looking younger than her age of thirty-something. He found it difficult, too, to see that such a young woman could provide a work he considered to be so important. He was totally surprised. He took an immediate and deep liking to her and they remained friends until his death in 1935 despite her move to America. Annie, often cynical, sarcastic, high-strung, and philosophical, but strong and determined, was very pleased by this honor and achievement and considered it one of the greatest thrills in her life. Overnight she became a painting celebrity. The contest prize provided an entrée into art shows in Berlin, and throughout Germany, too, without the required pre-screening by juries. She was now on her road to acceptance as an artist while her husband was making his way too. This may have been the start of their eventual separate yet parallel lives spent during forty-plus years of marriage.

While his wife established her own reputation as a serious painter, Alexander continued to implement his career and writing. He soon began to receive recognition as a rising star. In 1923 he won the first Freud prize for his work on *Castration Complex*. A series of his lectures, presented soon after arriving in Berlin, became his first book, *The Psychoanalysis of the Total Personality*, published initially in German in 1927 and then in English in 1930. His first book was praised by Freud, and Alexander continued to apply his theories of psychoanalysis when working with criminals. He was eager to understand the criminal personality and to apply psychoanalytic techniques to this social problem. These interests may have been an attempt to continue the ages-long dialogue with his father about philosophy and psychoanalysis.

Alexander travelled to Vienna many times a year to see Freud who was always enthusiastic to see him. They developed a confidence in one another and a meaningful friendship. Alexander would say that Freud spoke openly about his confidence in him during their visits together.

Anita in studio.

Freud, in one of the Freud-Alexander letters, wrote, "All of us count on you as one of our strongest hopes for the future." In the earlier Berlin years Alexander noted he had no desire to "run independent" as discussed in the Eissler interviews. He initially wanted to learn Freud's techniques and was practising like a classical analyst. He felt nothing but respect for the old master. He then, in part, may have begun to depart from his lifelong idealization of his philosopher father as he accepted Freud's views, as if a second father figure in his life. Additionally, Alexander considered Freud's psychoanalytic ideas to be the perfect vehicle for him to deal with his inner conflicts regarding his own father and his longstanding sense of poor self-esteem. A resolution of his internal conflict occurred when he accepted psychoanalysis. It was almost immediately thereafter that his first creative burst of writing took place. With his inner demons gone, his energy and commitment to work was boundless. Freud encouraged him to continue writing and thinking about his psychoanalytic ideas.

Eventually Alexander came to the attention of others in the psychoanalytic circles. It was only in the later years in Berlin that he began to think of separating from Freud and he started to experiment. He described Freud as having minimal expectations for change in therapy, unlike his own views. He said Freud often offered suggestions and gave advice to patients. He would say, "Try this," and on one instance Freud told a patient to get married. According to Alexander, Freud was eclectic and rarely followed his own rules. Freud did believe, though, that an analysis should end, ideally, with a transference cure. Alexander said that the group in Vienna was under the spell of Freud's personality and, although he admired Freud, he did not feel the same blind loyalty.

It was in Berlin where Alexander met Karen Horney. Horney was another pioneer analyst, and their effect on each other's professional lives would turn out to be far-reaching though not always positive. She was already practising in Berlin as a psychoanalyst when he entered the institute. She was not his first choice, but he would ask her to join him in Chicago as the institute's first co-director, a decision that proved to be unsuccessful and unsatisfying for both of them. Despite Freud's warning to the contrary, Alexander offered the position to Horney anyway, because he admired her keen scientific mind. The term was to be for three years. In the end, after a disastrous collaboration together in Chicago, Alexander agreed that Horney was a poor choice. Alexander stated that Horney's irrational hatred of Freud was displaced on all men and that this hatred of men made it impossible to work with her. In a conversation with Alexander, Horney agreed with his assessment and acknowledged her biases. She spoke openly of her abusive Norwegian father and her propensity to see all men as her father. Alexander would ask her to leave Chicago and Horney then went to New York. She had only spent two of the three years in Chicago. Alexander would later write to Freud and tell him he was right, she was unworkable, and he had made a mistake to invite her to come to Chicago (Alexander & Eissler, 1954). He would no longer feel the need to have a co-director at the institute.

In 1927 Alexander was able to spend some time with his father and they vacationed together in the small French town of Barbizon. The two walked and talked and enjoyed each other's company. Alexander, upon completion of his first book, gave the manuscript to his father to read and critique. He tells the story in *The Western Mind in Transition* of how his father came to appreciate Freud and the underpinnings of psychoanalysis. He wrote on the manuscript, "Your philosophical background allowed you to express those things more logically and simply" (Alexander, 1960, p. 56). He said that perhaps psychoanalysis instead of philosophy may bring about a new empirical approach to the study of psychology. As the father and son walked the trails in the nearby forest, it seems they came to a quiet and comfortable understanding. It may have been their last time together.

Bernard Alexander died in his sleep, at home in Budapest, on October 27, 1927. On his nightstand the latest edition of *Almanach der Psychoanalyse* was found. The professor father had just published an article on psychoanalysis which, it turns out, he wrote while on vacation with his son in France months earlier. In the article he wrote and compared Freud's repression theory with Spinoza's concept of emotions taking a second seat to intellect.—Bernard Alexander was almost seventy-seven years old when he was able to appreciate Freud. He had overcome his own inherent resistance as well as thousands of years of intellectual bias to get to that point. His brilliant mind allowed him to make the journey as well as his love for his son. This tender story is told with deep affection and uncharacteristic emotion in *The Western Mind in Transition*, and shows again how very important the connection between father and son was to each of them. Hundreds of friends and students took part in Bernard's burial in the Kozma Street section (Jewish section) of Rákoskeresztúri Cemetery in Budapest.

Another important issue that would consume the Berlin Institute for years was the issue of lay analysts. This would continue to haunt Alexander for decades to come. As is often the case, a patient was dissatisfied with the outcome of treatment and sued Theodor Reik. The patient claimed that his analyst had caused him severe psychological damage. Freud wanted to support Reik and wrote a booklet, *The Question of Lay Analysts* to do so. Freud believed Reik to be competent; he believed in lay analysis and had allowed a lay analyst to join the Secret Committee years before. Rado, Deutsch, Horney, and Sachs joined in the debate. The issue caused a near split in the community: Freud was in favour of lay analysts; Eitingon, along with the American analysts, was not. The opposing group wanted all analysts to have a medical background. A committee was formed to suggest an appropriate training protocol and to come to a negotiated truce.

In the late 1920s, William Healy came to Berlin to discuss the book on criminal psychology that Alexander wrote with Hugo Staub, *The Criminal, the Judge and the Public*. Alexander had begun a series of lectures on criminology for lawyers and judges. Dr. Healy, a pioneer psychiatrist and criminologist, had established the first child guidance clinic in the United States in 1909. Hugo Staub had been Alexander's analysand in Berlin and after the analysis was complete, they decided to pursue a social friendship. In fact, in the Kurt Eissler interviews, Alexander admits that Staub became his best friend and throughout their relationship, after the analysis was complete, they continued to discuss the lingering issues of transference and countertransference and their effect on the friendship. Alexander came to the conclusion at that time, and after his failed analysis with Freud's son, that it was impossible to analyse a close friend or one with whom you had a strong connection. He considered the analysis with Staub as well as Freud's son Oliver to be incomplete.

Healy was interested in the role the superego played in crime. Healy and his collaborator said that the commitment of crime in the United States was different than in Europe; it was more of a social phenomenon than an individual's act. It was perhaps the beginning of what we now identify as one of the social determinants of health that can contribute to social dysfunction and criminal behaviour. Healy and Alexander developed a mutual respect and Healy wondered if Alexander could sometime come to America and discuss the differences between criminology in the US and Europe.

Berlin in the late 1920s provided everything the Alexanders wanted: a good school for their firstborn daughter, Silvia, who began elementary school in 1926; fine restaurants and opportunities for music, opera, and art. As Alexander's life in Berlin continued, he seemed to experience the city as less uncivilized. Alexander was now making a comfortable income and the family had a nanny for the two young daughters. Entertaining was done at home, often, and lavishly. This apparent German financial prosperity, seen around them in society, was superficial and had been brought about as a result of the government's ability to float loans to pay huge war reparations. Most Berliners continued to party to excess and politics was not important to them. People had suffered during the war; now they wanted to enjoy themselves again.

The institute soon ran out of space and moved into new offices in early 1928. Freud's son Ernst was again commissioned to design and complete the new space at 10 Wiechmannstrasse.

In the winter of 1929 another depression hit the world, the stock market fell in the United States, and Germany again was in financial extremis. Foreign loans were called in, unemployment rose, businesses went under, and the mark again plummeted. The institute and its staff members, characterized by insulation and isolation in the past, were no longer immune to what was happening outside their doors. Eitingon's financial resources in the New World were no longer available to him and he was unable to pay the bills. Analysts often took reduced pay or were asked to reduce their caseloads. Additionally, many of the would-be analysts had trained elsewhere; they were labelled wild analysts, yet were seeing patients and thus diverting patients from the Berlin Institute. The Weimar Republic came to an end in 1931.

In 1930 Alexander was invited to come to America, to attend the meeting of the International Congress for Mental Hygiene. This meeting would turn out to be an important one for many people. Alexander was asked to present a paper on his work done with Hugo Staub. This work was an attempt to use psychoanalytic theory to describe the criminal behaviour of delinquents. It discussed the psychology of the judge and the jury. While still in Berlin, as a training analyst, Alexander knew many Americans and saw them as different from their European counterparts. He found Americans to be more tolerant in their opinions, more willing to accept the opinions of others during heated discussions. He was eager to go.

The twentieth century is largely considered by historians to be the American Century. America's chapter in world history as the most powerful country began before 1914, and its decision to enter World War I, against its own history, in support of the Allies, was a huge success. Subsequent to the war, unlike the European countries, America saw immense power and prosperity, leading to the first wave of immigrants who came to its shores and who were immediately assimilated. The ideals of personal freedom, liberty, and security were intoxicating and attractive to all who came. As immigrant populations grew, however, politicians and others began to speak of the need to close the open door to immigrants and to return to normalcy. Two immigration bills were passed and despite the warnings of President Woodrow Wilson, the country was on its way to isolationism. Quotas were instituted with a particular emphasis to control the numbers of immigrants coming from Eastern Europe. Through it all, despite its developing separation from the world, America would now influence Europe: with fashion, art, music as the Jazz Age exploded, and in film.

When Alexander came to attend the meeting in April of 1930, his work had preceded him. Immediately upon his arrival in Washington, he was impressed with the immenseness of America where everything was bigger and grander. The meeting was attended by more than 4,000 participants and was run with skill and finesse. Alexander remarked about the organizational skills that Americans had. Everything he encountered was magnificent. He felt genuine hospitality and welcoming from all the participants. His paper discussing the unconscious motives of criminals was discussed by Dr. Karl Menninger who challenged the psychodynamic views presented. Ironically, in the next two years, Alexander and Menninger would come together in their viewpoints and Menninger would be given the first training certificate from the new Chicago Institute.

Alexander was especially impressed by the willingness of all to try new ideas. This was a new experience for him and, as it turns out, quite intoxicating. This acceptance and encouragement of new ideas continued to be important for him throughout the rest of his life.

By this time Alexander could see that the massive capacity for organization, as well as the lack of political upheaval in the United States, made it inevitable that psychoanalysis would shift its center of power from Europe. It was at the International Congress meeting that he received a telegram from Robert Hutchins, the president of the

University of Chicago. Apparently Harry Stack Sullivan had already travelled to Berlin to check Alexander out and to make sure he would be a good fit for Chicago and the newly emerging field of psychoanalysis in that city. Mr. Hutchins was very impressed with Alexander and he, along with Dr. Franklin MacLean, the president of the University of Chicago Clinics, offered him a position as professor of psychiatry at the University of Chicago Medical School.

Analytic interest in Chicago began about 1921 with Lionel Blitzsten, who was an analysand of Otto Rank and who was a first president of the Chicago Society, and he had a loyal following that was offended when Hutchins made the offer to Alexander. Ernst Jones wrote that Blitzsten was the only psychoanalyst west of New York at the time and might have considered Alexander an intruder or carpetbagger. It was as if Alexander's eleven years and his accomplishments in Berlin were being denied outright. Alexander rejected Hutchins's offer as he felt the offer should instead be professor of psychoanalysis. His lifelong goal was to integrate psychoanalysis and medicine. Hutchins reluctantly agreed to change the appointment to visiting professor of psychoanalysis, in order to accommodate Alexander, and the offer was accepted. Alexander sent a telegram to his wife advising her of the offer and his decision. She wrote back with enthusiasm at the thought of living in Chicago. "By all means accept. I want to meet my infamous countryman Al Capone." (As an aside, a few years later Alexander would take on Al Capone as a patient.) She wondered, though, if people walked the streets with guns on their hips like in the Western movies. She often spoke of going to Chicago and "Wild-Westing it."

During the years primarily spent in Berlin, Alexander's identity as a psychoanalyst was being formed and he was becoming clear about where his interests would take him. He would leave behind everything he knew: a lifestyle, an important career where he was established, and a connection to his family. He still had his most important asset: his inquisitive mind that searched for new ideas. That quality he got from his father who stressed for him the importance of intellectual pursuits.

America was going to test his mettle and prove how stalwart he was. During visits and in correspondence, Freud warned Alexander about America and spoke openly of his distrust of America in many of the more than twenty Freud-Alexander letters. Freud hated America and that was no secret. Freud considered America to be too materialistic. Freud said Americans were only interested in money and publicity. Freud worried that America would "ruin Alexander" who he considered to be brilliant and "one of our strongest hopes for the future." Freud worried that America would dilute his ideas. One wonders if Freud was worried that Alexander, with distance between them, would become less loyal to him. Alexander said in the Kurt Eissler interviews of 1954 that Freud could not understand why he wanted to go to America "with the Dearborn Indians" and that America would be a "negro republic" in fifty years. Freud's hatred of America was irrational and Alexander disregarded the warnings. And besides, he had had an important dream and when he awoke he decided he must choose independence and leadership.

It was 1930 and the exodus from Europe of psychoanalysts was not yet in full swing though it is clear that Freud must have seen it coming. The appeal of the New World, with its promise of new ideas, was just too enticing and intoxicating to ignore. The tide was turning. The European migration was about to begin as anti-Semitism in Europe was again rearing its ugly head. Alexander boarded the SS *Bremen*, a new luxurious cruise ship, and sailed the Atlantic into New York harbour. His wife and two young daughters accompanied him on the voyage and began their new lives in Chicago at 5638 Dorchester Avenue. The adjustment to school in America was not uneventful for Silvia. The family spoke German at home and she knew no English. She was held back when she entered Girls Latin School and after one semester, rejoined her age group. Alexander assumed the post of the very first visiting professor of psychoanalysis anywhere, in America or in Europe. In Berlin he had established himself as the first trained psychoanalyst in the world. In Chicago, this pattern of trailblazing would continue.

Alexander's first appointment in Chicago was a near failure. His reception by the medical school was less than tepid. The medical schools in the United States, like their European counterparts, exhibited fierce opposition to psychoanalysis. The topic of psychoanalysis alienated the medical school faculty who considered it not scientific and likened it to a cult. The staff did not trust what was being said. It is, perhaps, that they were overly defensive as they attempted to become more scientific in their practices and teaching. It may be they suspected Alexander was Jewish, as were most European analysts, and the medical school in Chicago was deeply anti-Semitic. If he was questioned about being Jewish, Alexander would have denied it. Stella Moore, the daughter of Alexander's youngest sister, said that Alexander and his younger brother Paul once spoke with Lilla, her mother, and declared if she told anyone they were Jewish, they would kill her. While it is completely unlikely that either would have done anything so drastic, it speaks to their intense feelings of desperation, paranoia, and fear. Alexander's greatest secret, passed on from his father before him, was that he was Jewish. It was his dreaded fear that anyone socially would find out this secret. It may have been self-loathing. In fact, the secret was held by all his siblings and none considered themselves to be Jewish with the exception of Borka and her descendants. Alexander was raised a Roman Catholic, along with his siblings; his wife went to mass daily, and he did not consider himself Jewish, or at the very least, wished he was not. He had seen the repercussions associated with his father's university appointment and the covering up of distasteful family secrets, and the incident impacted him greatly. Oddly enough, years later, another director of the Institute in Chicago, Heinz Kohut, would also deny his Jewishness though, unlike Alexander, Kohut did have a bar mitzvah. It is clear that accepting one's Jewish heritage was not only a struggle played out in Alexander's family. It is a struggle for many.

In America, unlike Europe, the medical profession had to contend with the public and its influence. In Europe, professors were treated like kings, and were allowed to operate independently and without public scrutiny. In America, however, the public demanded to be informed. Alexander soon recognized this inherent difference between Europe and the US and knew that this kind of public pressure would impact the future of psychoanalysis in America. The very nature of the way in which America became an independent nation contributed to its potential mistrust of government officials and the need to keep a watchful eye on its fields of endeavors. There was no blind confidence as seen and felt in Europe, a sort of carte blanche for politicians and the government, and during the first years in Chicago this important lesson was presented for Alexander to learn. He did learn the importance of community partners and the benefit of lay people, and would apply these lessons to the policies at the Chicago Institute. It turned out to be one of his greatest contributions and it assured for him success at the institute as well as assuring continued success elsewhere. His unique decision to have a lay board in Chicago is still considered one of his greatest contributions. Nowhere was it done at the time; now it is commonplace.

As part of the position of visiting professor of psychoanalysis, the first ever in the world, at the University of Chicago's newly established School of Medicine, Alexander was to deliver a series of four lectures on psychoanalysis. He may have thought this was the beginning of his dream to unite psychoanalysis and academic medicine. He found, however, that the medical community was not in sync with his ideas. During an initial lecture in 1930 he discussed a woman who was suffering with constipation. He told of how he instructed the woman's husband to bring her roses and she was then cured. Most in the audience were outraged by Alexander and quickly turned on him.

During his first year in Chicago, the lectures given to lawyers and social scientists, on the other hand, were hugely successful. The halls were overflowing and everyone loved Alexander, who spoke with confidence and charm. His public lectures, in a hall of the Art Institute, were filled to capacity and so successful the money earned at the door equalled his salary for the period of his visiting professorship. It appeared that apart from the medical community, the rest of the town was ready to accept psychoanalysis and to embrace him. Alexander believed that the strident position taken by the medical community showed a distinct lack of understanding on their part of the philosophical principles of science. These differences reflected the different teaching strategies in America and Europe.

The final straw, however, may have been when Alexander saw a medical student for a long period of time, in psychoanalysis, charged a fee, and pocketed the money. He was also thought to have seen and charged students for supervision. The newly opened medical school, following the lead of Johns Hopkins, insisted faculty members must be full-time professors/instructors and its policy disallowed private practice. By charging private fees, Alexander was seen as unethical. Never mind that the treatment and/or supervision occurred over months and months, three or four visits per week, and that the idea of not charging for psychoanalysis did not make sense. He most likely was expected to offer professional courtesy to all those who were seen.

Overall, Alexander was treated rudely by the medical school. He was not behaving as others expected. He was, however, during that time able to focus on his work anyway and successfully completed the analysis of at least six or eight training candidates, and in 1931 he formed the Chicago Psychoanalytic Society.

The antagonistic reception he received in Chicago was not anticipated, especially after the warm welcome in Washington a short time before. Alexander left Chicago in disgrace and with profound disappointment. He had believed that America was ready for psychoanalysis. He returned to Europe and at that time he had no intention to return to America or to think it would eventually become his permanent home. He was then about to turn forty years old; certainly not the age when one considers such a major change. But Alexander was clearly different from most men. He was curious and he was ambitious. As it turns out, he was not through with America.

In 1931 Alexander returned to the United States and settled in Boston for a year and worked at the Judge Baker Foundation. His work there was supported by the Rosenwald Foundation. Also, Dr. Ives Hendricks, a newly trained analyst, asked him to assume the role of training analyst for the Boston Psychoanalytic Society. Hendricks had travelled to Berlin and had been Alexander's analysand. The Boston analysts began to fight among themselves along theoretical differences. Professor Murray, a psychologist and lay analyst, resigned from the society, a group he founded and what he considered to be in a hostile state. Many were asked to resign and reapply for membership after they had been "regulated" or made right with another analysis. Alexander conducted many of these analyses. During the year he spent in Boston, Alexander began an analysis of Henry Murray. The analysis lasted nearly a year and after Alexander left Boston and returned to Chicago, Murray accompanied him to complete the analysis. When Hanns Sachs came to Boston to train analysts in 1933, after Alexander left, his presence caused dissention as he was not a physician. Although Sachs had the blessing of Freud, as a lay analyst he was opposed by Hendricks. Interestingly, this issue of who should be trained as a psychoanalyst would become a thorn for many over the years and ultimately prove to be an important factor in Alexander's reluctant decision to leave Chicago for California after twenty-five years.

While he was in Boston, Alexander was contacted by Alfred K. Stern, an influential Chicago banker and the son-in-law of Julius Rosenwald. On behalf of the family's foundation he was asked if he would be willing to set up an institute for psychoanalysis modelled after the one in Berlin. As it turns out, Julius Rosenwald is Alexander's granddaughter's great-uncle's wife's husband's aunt's husband's aunt's husband's sister's husband's nephew's wife's brother (substantiated by the World Tree managed by Randy Schoenberg on geni.com.). It is doubtful anyone knew of the relationship, though distant, at that time. Stern believed that Alexander's apparent failure in Chicago was neither final nor complete. The Rosenwald Foundation had been set up by Julius Rosenwald and his family in 1917 and at its core was most interested in social issues. Rosenwald was a clothier and one of the founders of Sears, Roebuck, and Company.

As Alexander continued to help the Boston Society, his eventual return to Chicago began to preoccupy him. He settled the family in a four-story brick apartment building at 420 Memorial Drive, overlooking the Charles River, not far from the Massachusetts Institute of Technology and the Mass. Ave. Bridge. Alexander would see private patients in an office at home. He complained about the high rents in Boston when compared to rents in Chicago. The apartment building still stands and is an unassuming structure on the shore of the river yet comparable properties in 2014 sold for between $1.5 and $3 million. Life in Boston provided more luxuries than life in Berlin, yet the lifestyle was nothing compared to what Chicago would bring. For Alexander's firstborn daughter, Silvia, memories of life in Boston were vague but she did remember the address on Memorial Drive. Her parents enrolled her in the prestigious Beaver Country Day School, bordering the Boston suburbs of Brookline and Newton, which offered progressive education utilizing the country day school model. She summered that year on Cape Cod.

On March 1, 1932 the infant son of Charles Lindbergh was kidnapped from his home in New Jersey. Very soon after the Lindbergh kidnapping Mrs. Alexander received a note saying that her two daughters would be kidnapped unless a ransom was paid. She was terrified and took the girls to New York and ensconced herself in a hotel, most likely the Hotel Roosevelt where she had stayed many times before. She did not inform Alexander of her actions ahead of time and called him when she felt safe and secure again. Mrs. Alexander and the children remained in New York for several weeks and eventually returned to Boston. Alexander was left alone and how he managed is unclear. During the family's absence from Boston, Stern contacted Alexander and asked if he would set up an institute in Chicago, one modelled after the one in Berlin.

While in Boston, Alexander collaborated with William Healy on the psychoanalytic study of delinquency. Healy shared many of his ideas and they each advocated a multidisciplinary team approach to treatment, especially when working with offenders. They collaborated on a joint lecture presented at the Meeting of the American Orthopsychiatric Association in New York. Alexander had already written *The Criminal, the Judge and the Public* with Hugo Staub in 1932, and in 1935, *Roots of Crime*, co-authored by Dr. Healy, would be published after their work together. Both of these books reflected Alexander's interest in deviant behaviour. Alexander kept busy while in Boston and actually wrote one of his better books, *The Medical Aspects of Psychotherapy* … some wonder how he had the time to accomplish this.

One may consider his decision to return to Chicago as odd. He had been met there with anger and mistrust. At the end of his year in Boston, Alexander returned to Europe. Again he consulted with Freud and made the decision to return to Chicago. This decision showed, again, his tremendous courage to try something new, to venture to a new country, and spread psychoanalysis, but his version of psychoanalysis. Psychoanalysis would consume him. Freud asked him to remain in Vienna and to practise with him, but he refused the offer. Alexander said he did not think his future lay in reinforcing the fortress that was then around Freud, protecting him and his ideas. He did not think his life's work was to preserve Freud's work or his ideas about how to teach and practise psychoanalysis solely. He had ideas of his own and America was the place to take them. It was as if he was fulfilling his own manifest destiny. He would continue what he began two years before; he would move west. Helene Deutsch wrote at the time, "Immediate, well prepared success only fell to Alexander, who is esteemed much higher in America than Freud, and in spite of the bad lectures he gave he had a magical power that made all homosexual men in the highest places his slaves …" (Roazen, 1985, p. 275). Perhaps her statement is a bit overly enthusiastic and fanciful but it does represent the success he achieved. Franklin McLean said of him, prior to his invitation to come to Chicago, he was "unbelievably good."

Alexander knew that, with the financial backing of Alfred Stern, and a new institute that would be independent of the medical school, totally freestanding, he could return to Chicago as the conquering hero. And, he was right. He would gain respect from the community as he led Chicago through what some call "the golden years of psychoanalysis" as the first director of the Chicago Institute for Psychoanalysis and would remain at its helm for nearly a quarter of a century.

In Chicago, under his astute leadership, the institute would grow with his new ideas at the forefront. He never strayed from his ideals of being open to new ideas and David Terman, a Chicago psychoanalyst and a former director of the institute, said his legacy to the institute, and to Chicago in general, was his openness to new ideas, his brilliant scientific mind, and his commitment to research. The brilliant scientific mind, however, would first have to endure the challenges and the growing pains of the institute in its beginning years.

The family would undergo change and challenges as well, both in America and in Europe. By the time Alexander and his wife and daughters arrived in Boston, they travelled with a nurse/nanny for the two young girls. They stayed in the best hotels and bought expensive clothes and gifts from the best stores. One telegram from the period recalls trunks of clothing and furs put into storage at the request of Alexander's wife. As he prepared to leave Europe for the final time, Alexander contemplated the new world. America was enticing though in the midst of a depression; that did not concern him. He had lived through the financial chaos of Berlin. He knew the penny-pinching days of early Berlin were over, once and for all. The opulent days, reminiscent of his Hungarian youth and upbringing, would be the norm again. He was eager to move west, to America, to explore new horizons, new frontiers, and to attack new ideas with his undeniable and unending vigour and energy. He was filled with hope, but the transition from Europe would not be an easy one. First he and the family would spend the summer in the elegant resort town of Madonna di Campiglio, in the Dolomites region of Italy, not far from Lago di Garda. His sister Magda and her family would summer in the small Garda town of Malcesine and his mother-in-law, Guiseppina, was living in Milan at the time.

* * *

It is important to remember that America's influence around the world was becoming more and more evident; fashion, art, music and movies all helped to shape the world in the 1920s and beyond. English was replacing French as the so-called universal language due, in no small part, to the popularity of American-made motion pictures. The Alexanders would feel the need to be seen as American as soon as they arrived in Chicago. The need to assimilate into the upper middle class culture would again become important as it had been important to Bernard Alexander a generation before in pre-1900 Budapest. The

Alexanders would again reinvent themselves. And Alexander would keep to himself that his family was of Jewish descent. The irony is that although he never spoke of it, in public or with the family, everyone in the psychoanalytic community knew his secret. Apparently they enabled him and allowed him to maintain and believe the ruse.

CHAPTER SIX

Chicago and the time of his life

"We now feel we can cure the patient without fully understanding
what made him sick."

—Franz Alexander

When one considers Chicago in the 1930s several images
come to mind: the city's hustle and bustle, the Mafia,
political machines, the stockyards, gangland murders, cor-
ruption, and extreme weather—heat in the summer and blizzards in
the winter as the cold winds blow in off of Lake Michigan, showing
mercy to no one. All these describe what was happening in the city
on the lake that grew out of Fort Dearborn. Many of its early residents were immigrants and Chicago soon became the largest city in
the Midwest. During that time, because of the rise of the power of the
anti-Semitic Nazi regime in Germany, a significant number of analysts
fled central Europe and many came to America. Into this complex city
came Franz Alexander, a Hungarian immigrant, and his family. Though
Alexander never intended to return to live in the United States after his
first year in Chicago, he embraced his role as an immigrant with his
characteristic enthusiasm and vigor. Despite his being over forty years

old, Alexander's zest for life was unparalleled. He was optimistic about the move to America even though the country was in the grips of the Great Depression. He said, "I sensed the freshness of a youthful world, deeply involved in the problems of adolescence, full of energy, and yet, unsure of itself" (Levenson, 1994, p. 29). Alexander was ready for his next challenge: to spread the word of psychoanalysis. His mission now had a home: the soon to be opened Chicago Institute for Psychoanalysis at 43 East Ohio Street. Through the years the institute would have many homes before settling in 1992 at 122 S. Michigan Avenue. During the 1940s, when Alexander was the director, the institute was further up the street at 664 N. Michigan Avenue in a lovely eleven-storey Art Deco building built in the late 1920s known as the Farwell Building. The institute occupied the top three floors of this building. It was declared a landmark historical building and when the Ritz Carlton wanted to build high-rise condominiums next to it, in the early 2000s, the façade of the Farwell Building had to be taken down and reassembled.

Lionel Blitzsten and Ralph Hamill were both training analysts in Chicago before Alexander arrived. There is some confusion as to who analysed Blitzsten when he was in Berlin. Writings indicate he was analysed by Sachs or Alexander and there is some evidence to suggest he obtained later analysis by both Harry Stack Sullivan and Margaret Deri. He clashed with Freud in the early 1920s about not being on time for an appointment. A group of analysts and students began to meet regularly in Blitzsten's apartment and so began the famous informal seminars that continued for close to twenty years. Loyalty to Blitzsten was strong and during a history session at the American Psychoanalytic Association meetings in San Francisco in May 1982, where the Chicago years were discussed, some followers challenged the correctness of the title of a *Chicago* magazine article in September 1956 when Alexander's daughter called her father "The Man Who Brought Freud to Chicago." The panel included Douglas Orr, Jerome Kavka, Sanford Gifford, and George Pollock, with Felix Ocko as the chairperson.

Hamill welcomed Alexander's arrival to Chicago. "One might say, anything that Alexander said demanded acceptance" (American Psychoanalytic Association meeting, May 1982). He was confident and radiated positivity. When he taught, the students listened attentively. He commanded attention as any leader does. "It might have come straight from the mouth of Freud. And Alexander was wise and gradually talked the fundamentals of thinking and teaching of Freud. I can't remember his ever using his knowledge to belittle the efforts or thoughts of the rest of us" (American Psychoanalytic Association meeting, May 1992). Freud referred to him as "my best pupil in the United States" (Saul, 1964, p. 422) and remained in close contact with Alexander and was particularly interested in his career (Alexander & Eissler, 1954).

In a letter to Stern, dated December 22, 1931, Alexander clearly outlined his vision for the institute, evidently modelled and influenced by the Berlin Clinic:

> I am thoroughly convinced that our first plan was by far the most desirable in having an Institute consisting of two parts—an educational and a polyclinic—and gradually developing a third function—research ... We must have the attitude of giving competent treatment to everyone and the distribution of the cases is not dependent on the financial standing of the patient but upon other considerations such as the difficulty of the case, the experience or skill which the case requires, the special aptitude of an analysis for a certain case, etc. That is the procedure which we had in Berlin and it proved to be one of the great moral assets of our clinic which increased its reputation. (Schmidt, 2010, p. 75)

The institute in Chicago opened its doors on October 3, 1932. It was endorsed by the American Psychoanalytic Association that same year and by the International Psychoanalytical Association in 1933. Staff at the time included Karen Horney as the associate director, Thomas French, Helen McLean, and Catherine Bacon. Karl Menninger and Lionel Blitzsten joined the staff as lecturers. Chicago was the first and only foundation-funded institute with a salaried faculty. Because of this, Alexander believed his first important task as director would be to repair relationships with the medical community and to gain acceptance as well. In order to accomplish this very important goal, he dedicated himself to the area of research where he concentrated mostly on psychosomatic medicine. He also considered, for the first time, his ideas about a shorter analysis and may have been thought to be distancing himself and the institute from the classical Freudian concepts. Alexander would, however, iterate that his intent was to model the Chicago Institute after Berlin, and in 1956 he stated the goals of the institute were, in the early days, and at that time, the same as the goals of psychoanalysis everywhere: to provide treatment services to those who were suffering by trained specialists and to assure that services would be low-cost and available to all (Alexander, 1956b, p. 27).

Leadership came easily to Alexander and he gloried in the independence of the institute. The scars from the disapproval experienced at the hands of the medical community two years before still affected him. The original board of trustees, assembled by Alexander, included Stern, president; Sidney Schwarz, vice president; Dr. Ludwig Hektoen, noted pathologist, was treasurer; Mrs. Helen Swift Neilson, the heiress to the vast Swift meat packing fortune, and noted sociologist Professor William Ogburn. His plan to bring this diverse group together was another example of his openness to new ideas and his desire to rule in a democratic manner though some jokingly called him a benign despot. He was successful in obtaining funding from the Rockefeller Foundation and other institutions in order that the institute could teach, learn, and conduct research. Alexander so loved teaching and research and it is in these areas that his youthful enthusiasm and productivity came together in perfect harmony. Now in his early forties, he was about to scale even greater heights but those heights would not be reached without discord and more disappointment. Circumstances he disliked profoundly.

Alexander travelled to Germany to attend the 12th International Congress in 1932 where he reported on the progress to date of the Chicago Institute. He assured those attending there would be sufficient clinical casework for its students and trainees. He and Blitzsten were the only analysts qualified to do a training analysis at that time. When attending this congress, Alexander broached the issue of lay analysts and many in attendance were opposed to his ideas. Mostly the old traditionalists opposed him.

The air of dissent was insidious though hidden in Chicago as, on first blush, it appeared that Alexander, Horney, and Blitzsten were getting along and were in concert with their ideas. Karen Horney, however, soon began to favor the ideas and concepts of Blitzsten and she attended his seminars on a regular basis. As the meetings continued, Horney thought the attendees were suspicious of things German and thought psychoanalysis had been "Americanized" as Freud warned earlier to Alexander would happen. Now Alexander, ironically, was being considered by some to be a change-agent himself, a renegade, a maverick, instead of the one who was supposed to take psychoanalysis to America. As it turns out, he was both.

As Alexander continued to discuss and advocate his ideas to initiate a short analysis, and continued his psychosomatic research—he was, after all, a research man—Blitzsten and others began to question his actions. Blitzsten would not support the concept of a short-term analysis that focused on the patient's presenting problems. He preferred the traditional discovery of childhood issues that were gradually uncovered during a long analysis. A long analysis at that time meant sessions four or five days a week for more than 300 sessions. Alexander was proposing analysis three days a week. Blitzsten did not agree with the idea of using student-analysts and preferred that they be registered and fully accredited and at that time it meant through the American Psychoanalytic Association. He thought that discussing clients with lay analysts and students was unethical, as is customarily done in consultation and supervision, and to do so was a breach of confidentiality. Horney agreed with him. Blitzsten complained to the APA and, after a brief investigation, Alexander agreed to alter some of the new practices, for a while. Some say that Alexander soon ignored the need to change and, as a result, Blitzsten resigned his position at the institute.

Horney had been seen by Alexander when they were both in Berlin as "one of the most independent, skeptical, and questioning thinkers of the Berlin group," yet he came to think, in Chicago, she was unworkable, and "neither productive nor congenial" (Alexander & Eissler, 1954). By the end of 1934 Horney and Alexander were quarrelling and disagreeing more and more. They were totally at odds with one another. Horney was seen by Alexander as needing to control all situations as if acting out her relationship with her abusive father (ibid.). At the 13th International Congress held in Lucerne, at the end of August, Alexander announced that the partnership between himself and Horney had been dissolved. Despite this, they would remain friends and at future meetings could be seen talking or sharing a meal together.

Notwithstanding his break from Horney, and the departure of Blitzsten from the institute, Alexander continued with his agenda: To advance psychoanalysis through research; to establish and oversee a teaching program for psychiatrists to become analysts; to integrate psychoanalysis and medicine; and to provide the community an opportunity to understand and appreciate the field of psychoanalysis. Alexander considered research and teaching to be the most important purposes of the institute. His insistence that the institute be research-based was the avenue whereby psychoanalysis could be considered more mainstream and be accepted as a logical component of medicine. He thought that research and teaching must be linked together so that their inherent knowledge could be used in a preventive manner inasmuch as there were simply not enough analysts to cure all those who had mental health problems. At the time potential analysands were lining up to be accepted into treatment. The last item on his agenda was a natural outgrowth from his father's commitment to the concepts of the nature of man and the society in which he lives. Alexander was, indeed, his father's son and would have made Bernard most proud.

While Alexander was establishing himself as the leader of psychoanalysis in Chicago, his wife and children were becoming accustomed to their new home in a new country. Alexander's transition to Chicago and the closing off of his life in Hungary, and his ties to Europe in general, came easier to him than to his family. He was always searching for new places, new ideas, and this wanderlust continued throughout his life. He was intellectually restless and this played out as he moved from Budapest to Berlin, Boston to Chicago, and then on to California. It is likely that his desire for new things facilitated his adjustment to his many new homes. After arriving in Chicago, Alexander settled the family in an apartment located at 20 East Cedar Street, an elegant building with two-storied parlors, just around the corner from Lake Michigan. His acceptance of life in America would be so comfortable he would become a US citizen almost as soon as eligible, in 1938. His wife would not become a citizen for several more years. In fact, when she registered, as required, as a so-called enemy alien because of her Italian citizenship after the United States entered World War II, Alexander said that was horrible and "They will put you in a concentration camp and that will ruin me" (Alexander, 1987, p. 13). The family joked about the statement for years but Alexander did contact a friend at the Department of State, and his wife had her citizenship papers within a few short weeks. Alexander was also friends with President Franklin D. Roosevelt's Secretary of War, Henry L. Stimson, who had dinner with the Alexanders soon after the attack on Pearl Harbor in December of 1941. Stimson said at the dinner table that the attack was not a surprise and that, although the country was now embroiled in conflict in the Pacific, his concerns were more for Russia (personal communication, Silvia Alexander, 1987). It is interesting that Stimson was almost predicting the Cold War at a time when the United States and Russia were allies against Hitler.

The transition from Europe was bumpy and fraught with frustration for Alexander's wife and daughters as new customs and mores had to be learned and accommodated in the household. The girls were embarrassed by their parents` European accents and asked Alexander and his wife to stay home from school events. The children were enrolled in the Latin School (known at the time as Girls Latin School), a private school designed to provide its students with a college preparatory education that focused on the classics. Such a school most certainly fit into the mold of Alexander's classical gymnasium training and his many discussions with his philosopher professor father. Both girls made friends easily and became involved with sports, though Silvia not as involved as her younger sister Kiki. Alexander himself was an avid sportsman and on at least one occasion, during a blinding snowstorm, donned skis and made his way down Chicago streets to the institute. Silvia reluctantly played field hockey while Kiki played tennis and biked. Alexander took Kiki to the skating rink at the Lincoln Park Zoo, across the street from a later apartment at 2236 Lincoln Park West. Alexander enjoyed winter sports and had travelled to the Swiss Alps with his family many years before while growing up in Budapest. Silvia had trouble academically though not because she was not intelligent. She was more interested in her social life than in studying. During a final exam in history, she tossed a coin to assist her true or false answers on the test. Kiki, on the other hand, was an excellent student and achieved high marks. The Alexander children attended many of the analyst parties and congregated with the other children, playing on the beach, and going to the movies together. Dick Grinker remembered the Alexander girls well and how he and the children of the institute`s analysts would stick together at parties (personal communication, 1985). Kiki learned to dismantle a car engine in order to meet her father's need for a son and her need for attention from him. Their mother, Annie, no doubt drove them to school until they moved closer. She was an avid car enthusiast and owned many fast cars. She had a reputation of preferring to drive fast and always drove the family when they did not have a chauffeur or take a taxi. Alexander himself was a poor driver, a designation he readily accepted and never attempted to deny.

The family seems to have moved around a bit after their September 1932 arrival in Chicago. They left the Cedar Street residence and moved into the upscale neighborhood along the Lake Shore address and that then became the Lincoln Park West address. One thing is clear,

Left to right, Silvia, Anita, and Francesca Alexander, Chicago mid to late 1930s.

each apartment was located in what is referred to as the Gold Coast, the area south of North Avenue (1600 North) and east of La Salle and going south to about Walton St. It has a lot of the priciest real estate in Chicago. Apartments sold in these buildings in 2014 for two million dollars or more. The 1940 census lists the Alexander residence at 2236 Lincoln Park West and the household included live-in help. Silvia was away from home that year, studying at Mills College in the San Francisco Bay area for her first year of university, after graduation from the Francis Parker School in the summer of 1939. (One of Silvia's classmates was Nancy Davis, the adopted daughter of Dr. Loyal Davis, a Chicago physician. Ms. Davis would later become the first lady of the United States when her husband, Ronald Reagan, became president in 1980. Ironically, years later the author went to school with Reagan's daughter Maureen, whose mother was Jane Wyman and Reagan's wife before he married Nancy Davis.)

It is clear from these addresses that the Alexanders lived in the most desirable areas of Chicago, one might say, with the carriage trade. It is also clear that they had arrived, reinvented themselves, been assimilated, and were now part of Chicago's social elite. The building located at 1540 Lake Shore Drive was the only building on the lakeshore that was not restricted at that time, that is, the policies allowed Jews to live there. Is it possible that Alfred Stern, the first president of the board of the institute and Julius Rosenwald's son-in-law, had a hand in helping Alexander locate in those elegant quarters?

Silvia and her sister did not get along and their disagreements appear to be more than typical sibling rivalry. There was a near six-year span between them and their personalities and temperaments were drastically different, making closeness almost impossible. Silvia was fun-loving, superficial, and social. Kiki was studious and introspective. Silvia disliked discord and Kiki relished in discussing thoughts and feelings and liked the role of the intellectual child. In many ways, despite her younger age, Kiki bullied Silvia and played pranks on her that caused trouble between them and in the household. Instead of sticking up for herself, Silvia often took the path of least resistance and was passive. She admitted to being the instigator of the pranks when it was not true. Often the pranks were designed to get Silvia in trouble and they hit the mark. Perhaps Kiki was jealous of her older and more beautiful sister. Their sibling relationship would never be described as close, even in adulthood. Neither sister had truly positive comments to say about their childhood. Silvia once said she married her first husband, George Rotariu, the author`s father, in order to get out of the house which she described as rigid and oppressive. She sought to be more independent and to escape the rules that included curfews for her. She was rebellious and continued to act out her dislike of traditional family rules throughout most of her life. She never did what her parents expected of her and would be a disappointment and embarrassment. Kiki had troubled years and entered analysis with Dr. Albrecht Meyer.

Silvia saw Dr. George Mohr for a time after her marriage broke up. It is important to remember that Alexander was brought up in a professor's world where his father's word was the law. No doubt this influenced his parenting style and the way the household ran, even in America.

Alexander's wife, soon after arriving in Chicago, started to work on her art career. She joined the local art society, painted in her studio at home, took art lessons, and had many showings in New York and Chicago, one of which was a one-woman show. Alexander was proud of his wife's accomplishments and spoke glowingly of her work. At one opening gala he said, with enthusiasm, "I am the artist's husband." Mrs. Alexander was interviewed on the radio and for the newspapers and was considered to be a rising star with substantial talent. As Alexander devoted all of his time to psychoanalysis, Annie devoted her time to art, her new home, and the children. She felt abandoned and neglected, as did the children, who wished Alexander would spend more time with them. She had been raised in an aristocratic manner and was neither prepared nor groomed for marriage. She disliked being alone and wanted more of his attention. He tried to placate them but often felt ineffectual to meet their needs. He may have appeared nonchalant or disinterested. He had a mistress and that was his work. His concentration was elsewhere, mainly on his professional responsibilities and his patients, and the perceived lack of attention shown to his children was interpreted as disinterest or disapproval. He wondered how he could improve relationships at home, for there was often discord, disagreement, and dissatisfaction between them all, his wife and two daughters. He was left in the role of peacemaker.

Mrs. Alexander was left alone to manage the house and family and often had temper tantrums to get her husband's attention. Once during an argument she took a hammer to a delicate and beautiful bracelet of a butterfly encrusted with diamonds, other gem stones, and an opal for the butterfly body. She successfully smashed the bracelet. Her daughter Silvia recounted one important evening social engagement, in Chicago, when Alexander was confused and angry because his wife said she would not accompany him to the event. Silvia said to her father, in essence, "Of course she is going. She went to the beauty parlor and also bought a new dress." There was often drama in the household between Alexander and his wife though everyone believed they cared deeply for each other. One Christmas Alexander reprimanded Silvia for not writing a thank you note to her mother. Silvia, rather sarcastically, asked if the rule of etiquette applied to others as well, in other words, it is important for everyone to write a proper thank you note. He said, "Yes, it was proper." Silvia then asked why her mother did not write a note to her for a Christmas gift. Alexander said, "Well, that is different. You know Mama." He was always trying to navigate the minefield known as the women in his life: his wife and his daughters. Like Freud, he often would say he did not understand women yet had to live with them.

The Alexanders entertained a lot and, like the generation earlier in his father's house, most of the Alexander friends and colleagues were intellectuals. After the dinner meal, the men would retire to Alexander's study to discuss the important issues of the day and enjoy an imported cigar. The women joined Mrs. Alexander and undoubtedly discussed "less important" ideas. Mrs. Alexander could be flamboyant and excitable during these dinner parties. During one Thanksgiving dinner, she summoned the cook to "bring in the beast."

Alexander was soon accepted into the academic community and began to put his mark on it as well. Prior to leaving Chicago in June 1931, Alexander helped to found the Chicago Psychoanalytic Society whose charter members, other than himself, included Leo Bartemeier, Lionel Blitzsten, Hans Deutsch, Edwin Eisler, Alan Finlayson, Thomas French, Ralph Hamill, Helen McLean, Karl Menninger, George Mohr, and George Morgenthau. In 1938 he was appointed professor of psychiatry at the University of Illinois and he later organized the Associated Psychiatric Faculties of Chicago whose main area of interest was the psychoanalytic training for psychiatric residents. During this same time he was director of the Institute for Juvenile Research, associated with the University of Illinois, and founded by his friend and colleague, William Healy.

He was a man taught by his father to question and to think for himself. He encouraged and respected that in others. He was inquisitive. He was thoughtful. He was thought provoking. He was always searching for answers to age-old questions. He was willing to go in new directions for answers. One place he went for answers was to psychological medicine or psychosomatics: a field that, even today, is misunderstood. During his years as director of the Chicago Institute, he was dedicated to research in the field of psychosomatic medicine, perhaps to bridge the gap between medicine and psychoanalysis as a result of his initial reception in Chicago when a visiting professor.

In January 1939, a new periodical first was published, *Psychosomatic Medicine*, founded by Alexander and others at the Institute. Commenting on this publication, an editorial in the *Journal of the American Medical Association* paid tribute to the dynamic psychology of Sigmund Freud in its fundamental application to this new synthesis in medicine. No work on psychosomatic medicine could have been attempted without the biologically oriented psychology of Freud. Following his discoveries, Ferenczi, Abraham, Jones, Jelliffe, and more recently, Felix Deutsch, Wittkower, Menninger, Alexander and his associates at the Chicago Institute of Psychoanalysis, and Flanders Dunbar and her associates at the Presbyterian Hospital in New York, by their important researches, have added materially to our knowledge of this subject. (Blumenfield & Strain, 2006, p. 5)

From the beginning, Alexander wanted to experiment with psychoanalysis though he insisted he concentrated his efforts on practice, not theory. He always said he was not wavering from the basic concepts of psychoanalysis, namely that a "transference relation" be present in order for the analysis to be successful. This relation, he felt, could be best achieved if the treatment was adjusted to the individual needs of the patient. He was firmly committed to the concept of flexibility and believed that in order for psychoanalysis to be more broadly accepted, it must distance itself from its rigid practices of the past. It is possible that with Horney and Blitzsten gone, Alexander felt more able to experiment with the frequency of sessions, the length of treatment, and how the analyst conducts him- or herself in the context of the therapeutic relationship. It is true that Alexander had an ally in his colleague Thomas French, and their early work and research together would culminate in the 1946 publication *Psychoanalytic Therapy* that, interestingly, and surprisingly, would be thought of and criticized by purists as a repudiation of the concepts of Freud. In this book he proposed, for example, the concept of the "corrective emotional experience," a technique in which the analyst purposely behaves in the transference in a corrective manner toward the patient. For these ideas he was the leading figure of what came to be known as the "Chicago school of psychoanalysis," characterized by an emphasis on the emotional relationship rather than intellectual insight as the main curative factor. Alexander and Thomas, however, in the six or seven years before publication of their book, enjoyed success with the corrective emotional experience which was considered to be on trend at the time. The critical reception of these ideas would eventually be his undoing in Chicago and lead to his decision to leave the institute. This criticism came despite the fact Alexander was only attempting to initiate a discussion that is ongoing: What about the therapeutic relationship and process makes it work?

* * *

As Alexander fought a professional battle with his colleagues at the institute, and with the American Psychoanalytic Association, things at home were none too settled either. His first daughter married George Rotariu, a graduate student at the University of Chicago whose parents were not in the same social strata as the Alexanders. Silvia's parents did not consider George an appropriate choice for their daughter. Her parents were unhappy and her mother reportedly said, when she learned of the civil marriage ceremony, "For God's sake, don't get pregnant." Silvia and George moved into an apartment at 5468 Ridgewood Court in Hyde Park, close to the university, and according to George, were very happy. Silvia became discontent as her husband was balancing school and two jobs and was often not at home.

Silvia did, indeed, become pregnant and during the pregnancy was ill with toxemia or preeclampsia. She would be diagnosed with hypertension and manage the disease the rest of her life. Silvia was placed under medical supervision and entered Chicago Lying-in Hospital before her due date. Her daughter was born more than four weeks early and weighed less than four pounds. Both mother and child remained in the hospital though Silvia would go home without her daughter while she remained and continued to gain weight. Silvia and her husband named their new daughter Nina Alexandra, a name that Alexander would change months later when his granddaughter was officially baptised in Our Lady of Mount Carmel Catholic Church, 708 West Belmont Avenue, no doubt the church where Mrs. Alexander attended mass daily. Silvia left George when their daughter was about three months old. She divorced him in less than two years after returning to live with her parents. Alexander is known to have said, when he changed his granddaughter's name to his older sister's and his own, that if he was to support the child, he would name her. It is certain that this gesture, taking control in such a way, negatively impacted Silvia's sense of self, her ability to bond with the child, and her relationship with her father as well. Alexander inadvertently gave Silvia the message she could not do anything right, not even name her firstborn. Close to the time his granddaughter was born, Alexander suffered the first of two heart attacks. Cardiac problems and strokes are known to run rampant through his mother's side of the family and would affect some of his siblings too. Alexander spent time at the hospital associated with the University of Chicago and soon resumed his duties at the institute. He returned to his hectic work schedule and returned, as well, to his travelling and sports activities. He had also begun his role as father to Silvia's daughter, the author.

* * *

Kurt Eissler was most critical of Alexander and French's work and wrote, in his 1950 article, "The Chicago Institute of Psychoanalysis and the Sixth Period of the Development of Psychoanalytic Technique," that he had a difficult time understanding and comparing the

George Rotariu and Silvia Alexander on the University of Chicago campus, May 1944.

Alexander of that current day with the Alexander of the mid-1920s. He stated that Alexander had, indeed, fallen victim to what Freud had warned about: He had changed the concept and practice of psychoanalysis and discarded his (Freud's) works. "Alexander reverts to magical treatment couched in psychoanalytic phraseology when discussing the concept of the corrective emotional experience." Eissler concluded that psychoanalysis was in the midst of a crisis. A crisis brought about, according to Eissler, by Alexander and French's book *Psychoanalytic Therapy*. Eissler stated that "… crisis had been mainly limited to theory until now. Alexander's book initiates a new phase in which the crisis spills over into problems of psychoanalytic technique" (p. 40). He went further:

> Alexander's technique is, so to speak, a side branch … an attempt to establish the degree to which psychoanalytic knowledge may lend itself to magic psychotherapy. To be sure, this is a legitimate undertaking per se, but detrimental if done the way Alexander and his group did it. No doubt his technique will become the standard technique at the Chicago Institute … and have great appeal to the majority of workers in the field. It is short, it is less expensive to the patient, it is less painful for him, and it sounds more sensible than the "orthodox" technique. (ibid., p. 49)

He sardonically stated that shorter treatment and the corrective emotional experience would slay all the dragons that had previously been critical of psychoanalysis. Eissler seems to have been harsh in his criticism of the corrective emotional experience and his suggestion that history would not be positive in its assessment of Alexander's new ideas. Ironically, the concept of the corrective emotional experience has been accepted and is now conventional and the term has passed from psychodynamic to common parlance. The 1999 comedy *Analyse This*, starring Billy Crystal as psychiatrist Ben Sobel and Robert De Niro as gangster Paul Vitti, ends when Dr. Sobel says to his patient, "You can't say you were cured. Say you had a corrective emotional experience."

The years went on and eventually the ideas found in object relations therapy became popular at the institute. Some considered this was a rebirth of the corrective emotional experience. Finally it would appear that everyone paid attention to the importance of the patient's experienced emotions in analysis (Casement, 1990, p. 91), just as Alexander years before had suggested was important. The acceptance seems to have been a long time coming.

It is well known that Alexander liked to travel and he went abroad to Europe every summer. He often stopped off in Italy to see his niece Judith and had with him colleagues who included, in later years, May Romm, Sandor Rado, and Marie Bonaparte. Judith remembers that he was always surrounded by a lot of people, as if to buffer him from difficulty or intimacy. He travelled often to other major cities in the United States to attend scientific meetings and give lectures. He went to California once or twice a year to spend time at the house in La Jolla. There were those in Chicago who believed that Alexander's concept of the corrective emotional experience, and his interest in brief analysis, were together a mere attempt to suit his own needs because he loved to travel. It is difficult to accept this criticism inasmuch as he was so adamant that his children and granddaughter develop their own independence, not only in thought but in action. He so believed in the necessity to give back to society one's special gifts, be they artistic

Left to right: Father of the groom (Benjamin Thomas), bride Silvia Alexander, groom Douglas Nigel Thomas, parents of the bride (Anita and Franz Alexander), La Jolla, 1946. Alexander's daughter's second marriage.

creativity, a keen intellectual mind, or a commitment to hard work. It is this author's belief that those who were unable to accept him as the institute's director, for a long time, and who believed he was not loyal to Freud, were so conditioned to believe the worst of him, they were unable to accept any of his ideas as legitimate or useful. It is these very men who would also criticize him about his policy to support psycho-analytic training for lay analysts.

The stance of the American Psychoanalytic Association had always been that training be reserved for physicians only, and this usually meant psychiatrists. Freud long supported the concept of lay analysts and his Secret Committee included Sachs who was not a physician. It is also important to remember that Alexander had a positive experience during his short analysis with his lay analyst Sachs. European analysts and European thinking supported Freud, and also Alexander, but the Americans did not. As new theories and practices were coming to be more and more evident and accepted, the Americans demanded stricter controls on who could practise. It is ironic that they would do so as there were potential patients lined up for psychoanalysis at all the insti-tutes. There were more patients than could be managed.

This split in ideology spilled over into the Chicago Institute and Alexander found himself fighting a battle on two fronts: Short-term psychotherapy and the corrective emotional experience, and lay ana-lysts were the two issues and everyone took sides. It is ironic that, on the one hand, Alexander was being true to Freud regarding the lay ana-lyst training issue, and on the other hand was accused of abandoning Freud. He was caught between a rock and a hard place. One thing is clear, Alexander was considered by many to be a rogue and had to be stopped. Additionally he was described as an egotist who behaved as if "holier than thou" (Jerome Winer, personal communication, 2014). It is true, he was outspoken. His tendency to speak his mind must have been a threat to those who were still loyal to Blitzsten, many of whom had been analysed by him. The American Psychoanalytic Association, consisting mostly of traditional thinkers, is described as having been toxic at the time by some of today's psychoanalytic historians.

Juggling difficulties with his family, and at work, things came to a head on June 13, 1954, at 1:30 in the morning. While sleeping in their home at 540 Thornwood Lane, in the Chicago suburb of Northfield, Alexander and his wife were awakened by three armed men who broke into their home and robbed them. The robbers told them to put their hands behind their backs before they were tied up. Alexander carefully put one hand over the other and hid from sight a large star sapphire ring, one of his favorites. The top of his antique desk was ruined when the robbers gouged and cut it with knives. Mrs. Alexander was unable to salvage anything important when her bedroom was ransacked and precious jewels and cash were stolen. The jewellery stolen had a value at the time of over $7,000 and contained nothing but gemstones and 14 karat and 18 karat gold. Mrs. Alexander often told her granddaughter, the author, not to wear costume jewellery. She said, "If you can't afford gold and diamonds, don't wear anything." The loss was certainly not an insubstantial sum inasmuch as an average yearly salary in the United States in 1954 was $2,300.

The armed robbery, in the middle of the night, may have been the final attack that sent Alexander packing for the west coast. He had already been attacked by colleagues for his unpopular ideas and his attempt to bring about what he considered important changes to psychoanalytic technique and training. Therese Benedek said of him in a memorial service held in Chicago that "He appeared, always, as strong and invincible and, thus, an irritating target for counterattack." The robbery may have just been too much to bear, for both him and his wife. Suddenly the America that seemed so hospitable in 1930 was not so friendly any more.

After nearly twenty-five years at the helm of the institute, Alexander left Chicago with regret for California in 1955. He was dismayed and hurt by the reactions of colleagues regarding his ideas about short-term treatment and the training of lay analysts. He left behind some unresolved issues and he was succeeded by Gerhard Piers. Many analysts who had been influenced by Blitzsten were again the primary voices at the institute. The institute would reinstate policies that had previously been altered or challenged by Alexander. The Chicago Institute would enter a period of complete acceptance of the popular view at the time, of a deep and intense analysis, and not the short-term analysis proposed, supported, and researched by Alexander and French. This group of traditionalists was led by Maxwell Gitelson and the curriculum of the Chicago Institute emphasized a more traditional approach for the next ten to fifteen years. During the late 1950s and 1960s Alexander's name was rarely mentioned at the institute unless to be sarcastic and/or critical of the corrective emotional experience. Most certainly none of his writings appeared on reading lists for students or trainees (Jerome Winer, personal communication, 2014).

When his decision to leave Chicago was finally made, Alexander chose to spend a year in Palo Alto at the Stanford Center for Advanced Study in the Behavioral Sciences before going to Los Angeles. The experience was like going back to the days spent listening to intellectuals in his father's house: the coming together of diverse minds and opinions. It was energizing for him and he took that renewed rejuvenating spirit with him in order to forge new roads into the research of psychoanalysis and the therapeutic process in Los Angeles. He may have retired from the Chicago Institute, but he was most certainly not reducing his workload or limiting his interests or influence.

He always had a nostalgic feeling for Chicago and was somewhat wistful when discussing his former hometown. On many levels he regretted leaving his home of more than two decades, his friends, and professional relationships behind. He had, after all, spent the most productive years of his life in Chicago. He had always considered Chicago a "dynamic, progressive center of unlimited possibilities" (Alexander, 1956b, p. 31).

* * *

Four clinical psychologists filed a class action suit against the American Psychoanalytic Association in March of 1985. They claimed that the association and some of the training institutes had formed and established a monopoly and in so doing were complicit in their attempt to stifle competition. The lawsuit claimed the association was in violation of federal antitrust laws. The association denied the charges but a settlement was reached three and a half years later in November 1988. With the settlement the association agreed to no longer discriminate against nonmedical candidates who applied for membership and accreditation. The APA accepted the change and some said, after the settlement of the lawsuit, why did we fight so much? Many can no longer recall why they fought to exclude psychologists. All this happened just thirty years after Alexander left Chicago and twenty years after his death.

In a presidential address of the Academy of Psychoanalysis, published posthumously, Alexander said that the 1930s medical schools:

> … needed convincing that psychoanalysis belongs in their psychiatric curricula. Today, the psychoanalytic societies are the ones that are hesitant to relinquish control and direction of training in

psychoanalysis and relegate it to the traditional places in higher education—to the universities. I see as one of the functions of the Academy of Psychoanalysis to encourage this unavoidable process leading eventually to a unified, fully integrated residency training of psychiatrists, which would contain, in a single integrated program, both present day residency training and psychoanalytic training. (1964, p. 1)

* * *

At least in Chicago we, that is, the psychoanalytic institute, have some influence on some of the psychiatry residency programs, namely Northwestern, the University of Chicago, and Rush, and so those trainees still receive pretty good therapy training. And we have a small but steady stream of psychiatrists who come to the Institute for education in doing therapy. It's only fair that I admit that the narrowness and dogmatism of psychoanalysis especially in the Fifties and Sixties hurt it in psychiatry [sic]. The biggest factor in the United States is that psychiatrists can make far more money through prescribing than through doing therapy. (James W. Anderson, private communication, 2014)

In the 1950s there were twelve accredited training institutes in the United States, and in 2014 there are thirty. Today lay analysts are trained and accepted without bias and play a major role in mental health treatment. Change was slow, but eventually came to the field of psychoanalysis. In the end, Alexander's ideas and concepts regarding short-term analysis and psychodynamic psychotherapy are considered to be mainstream components of the armamentarium in the field and are practised worldwide by lay analysts who can now call themselves psychoanalysts. He was on the cutting edge of his field, always.

CHAPTER SEVEN

Moving west, one last time

"Say the French, 'See Paris and die!'
Make your home at La Jolla and live, say I."

—*The San Diego Union*, May 5, 1887

Just as Alexander did not know America would eventually become his home after his disastrous first year in Chicago, neither did he know that, while spending many summers in La Jolla, California would be his final home. Alexander started to travel west to California even before his wife bought two adjoining plots of land in La Jolla in the early 1930s. Soon after the Chicago Institute was up and running, the family took a summer vacation, in 1933, to California and drove, like many tourists, from north to south, taking in all the sights. The end of the road was, literally, La Jolla where the family spent many weeks, exploring the area that included trips across the border to Tijuana. On the train back to Chicago, Mrs. Alexander announced to everyone that she had bought some land and that in November 1933 she would return for the building of a new house. She fell in love with the charming little seaside village that reminded her of her native northern Italy near Venice and Trieste. Many of the trees and shrubs adorning the streets were reminiscent of the gardens she knew in the towns and villages on the Adriatic. She was comfortable and at home in this part of Southern California and without consulting her husband, she immediately purchased the land with plans to build a hacienda atop the hill that overlooked the Pacific. Alexander was surprised at his wife's independent actions. The children worried about who would care for them back home in Chicago when their mother was in California with builders and architects. Silvia and Kiki were still adjusting to the changes they had experienced in their young lives: First leaving Berlin to live in Chicago 1930–1931, a brief return to Berlin, a year in Boston 1931–1932, another trip to Europe, and finally the move to Chicago in late 1932. Alexander's wife took care of all the arrangements to make sure the house ran smoothly in her absence, and made sure she was back home in Chicago to celebrate Christmas with the family. The following spring, in 1934, the Alexanders' new beach house was completed and represented a welcome change from the formality of Chicago. Alexander enjoyed the casual lifestyle of La Jolla, was a sun worshiper, like his younger brother Pali, though he always made sure to do some bit of work daily wherever he was.

La Jolla house entrance.

La Jolla has its roots in art and before the turn of the twentieth century, was known for its artist colony. The primary benefactress of La Jolla was newspaper heiress Ms. Ellen Browning Scripps whose wealth helped to establish important buildings and parks before 1900. The Scripps Oceanographic Institute bears her name. In the days after World War I La Jolla's beach community consisted mainly of beach cottages that were neither large nor luxurious. The small houses dotted the cliffs near the ocean. The vast open lands were full of chaparral and horse trails ringed the mountains. It was not until close to World War II that La Jolla became a true tourist destination and the small cottages grew larger and took on the appearance of the sprawling Spanish hacienda. Returning soldiers took up residence in La Jolla and the population began to grow. The town, though, never lost its appeal or the magical feeling imparted to visitors and residents alike. Today about 40,000 people call La Jolla home including some of the Broessler cousins. This was a community where lifestyle was important long before the term existed in our modern lexicon. La Jolla was geographically isolated before the University of California at San Diego became a large campus and the town itself always remained bucolic. La Jolla was and is today the epitome of comfortable family living. It was a perfect fit for Alexander who grew up in a family that stressed vacationing together and whose children had been placed in rural country school settings.

The Alexanders' La Jolla home, at 5758 Dolphin Place, sits proudly perched atop the ocean on a bluff covered with succulents and cacti. After her secret purchase, Mrs. Alexander, feeling more at home as she was reminded of her home in Italy, near Venice, immediately engaged noted Southern California architect Cliff May to design a hacienda. His houses embrace the out-of-doors and have a distinct connection to the environment surrounding the house. The house was and is still a typical Cliff May, designed with the lifestyle of the family living inside taken into consideration. Alexander and his family loved California, the sunny days, the beach at their feet at the bottom of the cliff, and the relaxed feeling of being away from the hustle and bustle of Chicago. The Alexanders came to La Jolla every summer through the mid-1930s and into the 1950s, like so many others who called La Jolla their summer home.

The large, sprawling red clay roofed house had an enclosed central patio with thick walls covered with a crimson-colored bougainvillea, and a terraced garden with olive and pomegranate trees and a stairway down to the private beach. Alexander bought out a local tile company and designed the floors using the tiles. Mrs. Alexander planted many cacti in the front yard and they suited the natural look of the cliffs overlooking the ocean. The ocean views were spectacular, from each and every room, and the sun shone brightly on this house, all the time, at least in the author's memories. This house, and La Jolla, to this day remains for the author a beacon of good times and happiness for all who assembled there.

It is not surprising that the Alexanders were drawn to the community. Soon after the completion of their California beach house, the Alexanders were welcomed into the social scene. They joined the La Jolla Beach and Yacht Club, which had opened in 1927. Theoretically Jews were denied membership at that time, but Alexander and his wife told no one of his Jewish heritage. Frederick William Kellogg purchased the property on August 19, 1935, and together with his wife, another Scripps family member, Florence Scripps Kellogg, opened the club as an exclusive oceanfront resort. To this day, the club remains in the hands of its founding family, the Kelloggs. There were four tennis courts and a swimming pool at the newly renamed La Jolla Beach and Tennis Club. In 1931 the Children`s Pool and Seawall was constructed, in 1940 the art centre opened in the former home of Ms. Browning, and in 1942 the Balmer School, then to be renamed the La Jolla Country Day School, was opened. It seemed that the sleepy little village was being discovered and coming into its own; no longer considered just a suburb of San Diego.

Alexander loved La Jolla and his summers there. He enjoyed the climate and spent most of his time outdoors. He worked in the mornings only and then spent the rest of his day on the golf course at Torrey Pines with his oldest daughter, Silvia. He and his wife went to the racetrack at Del Mar where he was often successful using what he said was his own special scientific method of choosing the winning horse. He and his wife could be heard talking to themselves, adding sums, and calculating their winnings in their separate native languages: he in Hungarian, she in Italian. Alexander often played tennis with his youngest daughter, Kiki, at the beach club and swam in the pool as well. Evenings were spent entertaining friends or going to the movies. As soon as the Marine Room opened in 1940, an oceanfront restaurant adjacent to the beach club, the entire Alexander family would dine there several times a week during the summer months. Another favorite spot was Anthony's for Fish and the Top of the Cove on Prospect Street.

Abalone was a favorite menu item for all as well as mock turtle soup. Many times Alexander would barbecue his famous steak with a lemon and paprika marinade and he especially enjoyed sharing this meal with friends. He was an attentive and fun host and loved having friends and family in his home. Like his father before him, Alexander would offer cigars and a good sweet after dessert wine to his guests. Alexander gave seminars during the summer months, but mostly relaxed, wrote, and enjoyed being with the family. Mrs. Alexander became part of the artist colony and began to experiment in oil pastels. She hung some of her paintings in the local galleries and loved spending time, with her paints and easel, in and around the small beach town. This period may have been her most prolific painting period. The family took frequent trips across the border to Tijuana to eat and purchase crafts, silverware, and food. Alexander's granddaughter's sterling silver baby cup came from Mexico and she was often seen enjoying a special Mexican candy, *piruli*. Everyone loved La Jolla and many times the Christmas holidays were spent there instead of in the cold of Chicago.

Life in La Jolla was different from the more formal Chicago. In Chicago most of the Alexander friends and contacts were members of the intelligentsia, just as the friends of Bernard had been a generation prior. In La Jolla, Alexander was more relaxed, playful, and fun. His friends there did not fully accept or understand psychoanalysis yet and when he was introduced as a physician instead, the women would often ask him about their hypertension or headaches. He would play with them, teasingly, and mention that their ailments were due to repressed rage or sexuality. He was never more charming according to his children.

Kiki became friends with an older man across the street who would often babysit Silvia's young daughter. Kiki described this man as lonely and she decided to arrange a date between him and her sister. This man, Douglas Nigel Thomas, the son of Benjamin Thomas, was an aeronautical engineer. His father had come to Hammondsport, New York in the teen years of the twentieth century in order to continue to work on and develop his creation, the Curtiss JN-4 Jenny aircraft. This aircraft was used extensively during World War I and thereafter primarily as a training aircraft. Benjamin`s wife died when the youngest of the two sons was only three and he raised Douglas Nigel and his brother Malcolm alone. The family moved to La Jolla in the early 1940s and lived kitty-corner to the Alexanders, on Chelsea, in a more modest home. Silvia and Nie (short for his middle name, Nigel) became sweethearts and in 1946 they were married. Pictures of the bride, at her second wedding, were circulated to family members around the globe who all inferred it was her first marriage. None of the Alexanders said otherwise. Silvia's ex-husband, and father of her young daughter, was thereby erased. Unfortunately, so too was Ilonka erased from the family. Only a few cousins would know of the first marriage and the birth of Alexander's first grandchild.

In the mid-1950s, when Alexander made the decision to leave Chicago, it was assumed that La Jolla would be his primary home. Plans included he was to move into an apartment in Los Angeles yet his wife would remain in the beach house. Unfortunately, she began to experience the painful effects of arthritis, her fingers hurt most of the time, and she was unable to continue working on her painting and sculpting in the damp climate of La Jolla. They reluctantly decided to move inland, to drier air, and the house in Palm Springs was built after Mrs. Alexander hired Austrian architect Walter S. White, who had vague ties to Freud, to design it. He was an architect who specialized in modern desert residences. Typically, when designing a house, White's first concern was the roof and the angle of the house in relation to the sun. The roof had to protect the inhabitants from the heat of the desert sun which would exceed 110 degrees Fahrenheit in the summer months. Walls in Walter White houses were nontraditional in appearance and number. In Alexander's Palm Springs house the walls did not reach the ceiling and the spaces inside the rooms seemed to float one to another. One side of the house overlooked the valley of Palm Springs below and consisted only of glass. One entire side of the house, its entire length, was made of sliding glass doors and, like a typical Cliff May house, the outside was incorporated as part of the living space to suit the lifestyle of the owners. It is thought that she sought a new architect, with avant garde ideas, to design the house as it complemented her artistic creativity at the time reflected in her change in technique. Mrs. Alexander was commissioned to sculpt several statues for the newly opened Palm Springs Hotel and Spa. Mrs. Alexander's painting style was undergoing a drastic change as she began to exchange her brushes for palette knives. She would put paint on the canvas and work with the negative space and scrape the paint off. Alexander left all the details of the construction, decoration, and design to his wife and Walter White. They were both given carte blanche. Ironically, the Alexanders were dissatisfied with some things during the building process, and work had to be redone on walls and infrastructure. This house is now considered to be one of White's masterpieces and is located at 1011 Cielo Drive, nestled in the foothills at the bottom of the San Jacinto Mountains. Frederick Loewe, of Lerner and Loewe Broadway musical fame, lived next door.

In choosing this architect and accepting the blueprints and house plans, Alexander again showed the contrasting sides of his personality. He embraced the classics yet chose an ultra-modern house for a home and filled it with mid-century modern furniture while books, on all subjects, lined the walls of the living room, his study, and his bedroom, from floor to the top of the walls.

* * *

The beginnings of psychoanalysis in Los Angeles date to an informal study group in the late 1920s. By the mid-1930s a more formal group had been organized, interestingly, under the aegis of the Chicago Institute for Psychoanalysis. Ernst Simmel and Otto Fenichel came from Berlin, May Romm emigrated from Russia, and German analyst Frances Deri came from Prague where she was living when Fenichel was there. Both Fenichel and Deri were part of the Prague psychoanalytic group in the 1930s. As the storm clouds over Europe were darkening, a large group of Jewish analysts fled to avoid persecution by Nazi Germany. Some were not so fortunate and lost their lives at Buchenwald and Auschwitz. For some odd reason, once they arrived in America, the European Jewish psychoanalysts gravitated to California and in particular to Hollywood. There was a strange attraction between Hollywood and psychoanalysts who had busy practices and who were enjoying intellectual prestige in the City of the Angels. The Los Angeles Institute was founded in 1946 and the profession became popular, and analysts were in high demand, as elsewhere in the country.

From the beginning, however, tensions among members caused disharmony at the institute, not unlike the tensions experienced in Chicago between Alexander, Blitzsten, and Horney. As the issue of lay analysts almost tore apart the Chicago Institute and led to Alexander's desire to withdraw the institute from membership in the American Psychoanalytic Association, so too did the members in Los Angeles disagree. Some of the original and founding members in Los Angeles were not against lay analysis, but others, including May Romm and Martin Grotjahn, were vehemently opposed, with May Romm being the most vocal and vigilant. This issue, ironically, had been a thorn for many before the Los Angeles Institute was formally formed, and reared its ugly head when the European émigrés had to be retrained in order to comply with standards of practice in the United States.

A new group emerged from the conflict which called itself the Southern California Psychoanalytic Society and Institute. The split occurred in 1950 and the new group consisted of the medical analysts who were opposed to lay analysis. The Los Angeles Institute carried on with the original name and both were allowed membership in the American Psychoanalytic Association. Most of the European-educated analysts would pledge their allegiance to the Los Angeles Institute that did not forbid or disapprove of a nonmedical analysis. Interestingly, though, the majority of members were traditional analysts who practised and adhered to Freud's concepts and practices. The preponderance of its members was especially insistent on orthodox Freudian theory and technique. It is ironic that the medical group, the newly formed Southern California Psychoanalytic Society and Institute, embraced new ideas and those new ideas included the practice of short-term therapies and the "corrective emotional experience" advocated by Alexander. Ironic inasmuch as their willingness to consider new ideas did not include Alexander's and Freud's views on lay analysis.

During the 1950s both institutes grew and expanded in what was the heyday of American psychoanalysis in California. Being in analysis was popular and analysands often discussed their analysis in social settings. Psychoanalysis was made popular in a slew of motion pictures as well. May Romm worked with English director Alfred Hitchcock on his film *Spellbound* as a consultant. Despite being the upstart group, the Southern California Psychoanalytic Society and Institute entered a quiescent period and even relinquished its demand that psychoanalytic training be available only for physicians. In 1956 the Southern California group welcomed Franz Alexander, who left Chicago and moved to California in his final years. This move did not mean, however, that he was actually retired; his work in California consisted of establishing a private practice, research and administration at Mt. Sinai, and he was writing at least two books as well as teaching and giving lectures.

* * *

Alexander explained his decision to move to California as wanderlust. He was angry and disappointed that his colleagues at the institute in Chicago did not support his desire to leave the American Psychoanalytic Association over the lay analyst issue that erupted during the so-called crisis as described by Eissler. When he agreed to supervise Dr. Hedda Bolgar, a nonmedical analyst in training, during the early 1950s, he jokingly said it may get him into trouble. At the same time the offer came from Mt. Sinai Hospital to establish and manage a Department of Psychiatry and oversee research. It was a program that would be dedicated primarily to research and this excited Alexander. The offer came at a perfect time for him and was just too attractive to refuse. He was able to get a Ford Foundation grant to institute a program in psychotherapy and psychosomatic medicine at the prestigious Los Angeles hospital. The Ford Foundation funded the project for $250,000 which, in 1956, was impressive. In Los Angeles he would be able to study the psychotherapeutic process in a controlled setting, something he had wanted to do for quite some time. He said, "We can only teach what we know. I shall continue to study—I shall devote almost all of my time to further research, and to reevaluating those principles which I have been practising for thirty-odd years" (Alexander, 1956b, p. 31). He would come to realize that successful treatment depended 95 percent on the therapeutic relationship between patient and therapist, and 5 percent on insight or interpretation. This finding seems so obvious to psychotherapists now. In making such a statement, some wrote Alexander had stepped away from Freud. Some say he abandoned Freud. Erika Schmidt (2010) in her excellent review of Alexander and his time in Chicago comes to the conclusion that, indeed, Alexander remained true to the ideals and ideas of Freud.

After the year spent in Palo Alto, at the "think tank," Alexander was renewed and the experience of coming together with other like minds, in different disciplines, affected him greatly. He wanted to bring this newfound knowledge to psychoanalysis and the therapeutic process. He obtained grants from the National Institute of Mental Health which allowed him to continue his research. He was keen to share what he had learned and experienced with his colleagues. He was rejuvenated and eager to share updates with his former colleagues in Chicago when he visited.

Helen McLean wrote, "His constructive response of 'brief' psychotherapy was similar to his reaction to the hostility shown by medical colleagues in 1930. Earlier he had turned to a study of psychosomatic conditions; now he began a detailed, controlled study of the therapeutic process" (McLean, 1965, p. 249. Although he officially retired from the Chicago Institute when he moved west, he was by no means retired. His mindset would not allow for that. He always strived to achieve the next goal, his mind was never still, and he had plans and goals for continued work. He was his usual zestful and energetic self. He had plans to eventually live in Switzerland where he thought he might retire "at some time" and be able to sit in cafés, like his father before him, as in his younger years in Budapest, and enjoy conversation with friends and intellectuals.

* * *

With his wife in Palm Springs, and his daughters married or living back in Chicago, Alexander was alone to locate a place to live. He found an apartment in a hotel-apartment building on the Wilshire corridor between Westwood and Beverly Hills. He disliked being alone, eating alone, and was lonely all by himself. He was in a new city with new challenges: his family was not close by and he missed all of them. It was a new kind of existence. He often cajoled his colleagues at Mt. Sinai to stay late at the end of the day and join him for dinner. At roughly the same time, Silvia divorced her third husband, known in the family as George number two, and Alexander proposed a plan to make everyone happy. He asked her to move in with him, he would find a larger and more suitable place for everyone to live, and he would pay the bills. The arrangement sounded ideal to Silvia whose daughter Ilonka was now living with her and soon to start the tenth grade. No doubt Silvia was worried about financial matters and this was now no longer a concern. Additionally, the scrimping she may have endured during the marriage was over. She was again living in the style to which she had been accustomed during her youth and young adult days. Silvia was then just thirty-seven years old.

In the summer of 1959 Alexander and his oldest daughter and granddaughter moved into the duplex at 10952 Ashton Avenue in Westwood Village. Silvia found a new job at an agency catering to actors and other entertainers, and Ilonka began to prepare to start high school in West Los Angeles. It was the ninth move she had made in her life and these moves represented to Alexander instability he hoped to correct. It was not long before Alexander was fixing his daughter up with more suitable men and arranging dates for her. These men were doctors and psychologists who Alexander thought were a better match than the grocery store clerk she had chosen for her third husband. He was a loving father who was trying to help her in her search for the ideal husband. His efforts were not appreciated by his daughter who preferred to find her own partners and Silvia complained bitterly to her father about his interference. It was not the first time Alexander interfered with his daughter's relationships. Silvia would say to her daughter, decades later, that she regretted her decision allowing her parents to interfere with her marriage to Ilonka's father. "No doubt your life would have been better and more stable if I had not let Mama and Papa tell me what to do. I am sorry my choice made your life difficult." This insight and candor was the only such exchange between them.

The Alexander family, though, had ongoing challenges. Silvia and her sister were not friendly. Ilonka felt estranged from her mother and had lived apart from her mother most of her life. Alexander wanted desperately to bring together these disparate family members, all of whom he loved dearly, and he wanted to make peace. Since his daughter Kiki told him he had failed as her father during her teenage years, necessitating an analysis with Albrecht Meyer, Alexander was determined to create a better atmosphere for his granddaughter. Unfortunately, Silvia considered his behavior to be meddling and after two years together, cancelled their arrangement. For Ilonka it meant leaving the home she enjoyed and the attention and security she felt. For Alexander it meant, again, that he would live alone during the week. He sought and found an apartment at the Chateau Marmont in the Hollywood area and lived there until his death. He disliked living alone and attempted to fill as many hours with others as he could. He could be charming and engaging and it was difficult to deny him anything.

Alexander spent weekends with Mrs. Alexander in Palm Springs and often took his granddaughter with him. At home in Palm Springs, he and his wife entertained friends and cooked together. A favorite was Annie's gnocchi, a northern Italian potato dumpling served with a marinara sauce. Silvia and her daughter would often raid the icebox in the middle of the night and consume large quantities of gnocchi. These little dumplings, cold, were like cement hitting their stomachs but both delighted in the midnight meals.

Soon after Alexander and his wife moved to California his youngest daughter Kiki did as well. She often said she completed a long analysis in Chicago before venturing west. She joked that her twelve-year analysis did not fit into her father's mold of a short analysis. She was the last of the family to leave Chicago and make a new life in another part of the country. She piled precious belongings into her VW Bug and moved into a small cottage, again atop a bluff overlooking the ocean, in the affluent and conservative village of Pacific Palisades. She began her doctoral studies at USC and in her research work she studied the relationship between delinquent girls and their probation officers. During her research she met Jack Levine who was an assistant director with the Los Angeles Department of Probation. After a year or more they decided to marry and Jack went to Alexander to ask for his daughter's hand. Despite being at the forefront of psychoanalytic thought for decades, Alexander was a traditionalist when it came to family matters. Those old world values of the bygone era never left him when they involved his family. Jack did not receive Alexander's wife's blessings and she refused to allow Alexander to attend the wedding let alone give his daughter away. Alexander did not challenge his wife's decision and for that, he apologized to his daughter and new son-in-law later. Kiki's sister and niece were not in attendance either. Dr. George Mohr gave Kiki away to Jack in a Roman Catholic ceremony held in Corpus Christi Church in the Pacific Palisades. It is speculated, by family, that Mrs. Alexander did not approve of Jack because he was Jewish and, as a devout Catholic, she did not want to acknowledge another Jew in the family. She and Alexander had done their level best to deny his Jewish heritage for many years and had been successful, at least socially and in the family. Eventually all of the Alexanders, and Jack, became friends and were cordial to one another.

In the summer of 1962 Alexander's daughter Silvia married for the fourth time. She married a chartered public accountant with whom she worked together in the home of former film star Mary Pickford. Silvia had known Fred Dodge for several years and her dating habits were often grist for the mill when she fought with her father about what time she should be home with a teenage daughter at home alone. Fred accepted a new post in Reno, Nevada as the CPA for E. L. Cord, an auto designer and financier, who owned the NBC affiliate. Fred and Silvia moved the first of July 1962 and Ilonka moved in with her aunt Kiki.

Alexander's lifelong dream to establish a professor of psychoanalysis at a university was realized when the University of Southern California established the Franz Alexander Chair of Psychoanalysis in the School of Medicine and he was the first appointee. He spoke with eagerness about this new achievement to friends and family. All his life Alexander

Palm Springs house.

hoped to be an academic, like his father. This wish is an example of what Bernard said to his son when he accused him of trying to compete with him. It certainly shows the need of Alexander to impress his father and obtain his acceptance. A need and desire that is totally understandable. He was finally able to achieve this goal. Alexander died after achieving this long wished-for dream though he certainly had many more worlds to conquer and dreams to fulfil.

Alexander died in his Palm Springs home on March 8, 1964 after a brief illness. It was the day before his wife's seventieth birthday. His family was stunned and heartbroken. The psychoanalytic world was shocked to hear of his death, a man most considered too young to die, despite his being seventy-three years of age. His death was more shocking in that he was scheduled to give the Karen Horney Memorial Lecture in New York three days later. Those attending the funeral mass in Palm Springs are too many to list, but included Sandor Rado, Bruno Bettelheim, Karl Menninger, Heinz Kohut, May Romm, Roy Grinker, Thomas French, Hedda Bolgar, George Mohr, Judd Marmor, and on and on.

Helen Ross, the administrator of the Chicago Institute, described Alexander as the "playboy of the western world" and that most assuredly speaks to his playful, youthful exuberance for life. He was, though, and remains, a man few knew. He is a man who touched many lives, who created controversy in his attempt to challenge ideas, and a man who lives today through his works and the changes that have occurred in the field, changes he thought necessary and for which he took a stand. A notable authority on Freud, Alexander considered it essential to elaborate on Freud's ideas, viewing disturbed human relations, rather than disturbed sexuality, as the main cause of neurotic disorders.

* * *

He believed himself his mother's favorite; certainly, he was beloved and needed by all who knew him ... Martin Grotjahn.

He will be greatly missed by those who appreciated the brilliance of his thought and expression in all the areas of psychoanalysis to which he made contributions ... William Silverberg.

He made students of us all ... Sheldon Selesnick.

The world lost one of its foremost psychoanalysts. I lost a lifelong friend ... Workers in all these fields may long be expected to feel his influence ... Sandor Rado.

Alexander followed what Freud quoted at the end of his "Outline of Psychoanalysis": "What thou had inherited from the fathers, acquire it to make it thine." He mastered it and made it his ... Alexander showed only tolerance, understanding, and unfailing kindliness. He was a big and broad person—in his abilities and in his feelings for people. He enjoyed life to the full in every area ... Freud chose well when he invited Alexander to be his assistant ... Leon Saul.

Alexander was the paradigm of the scientist philosopher and the philosophical scientist ... Carl Binger.

He served as a catalyst for investigation and synthesis of new concepts ... He was brilliant ... We have suffered a great loss ... George Ham.

It is clear that Alexander was a man of creative imagination, boundless energy, and a productive professional life. His works and writings were rich and fulfilling. He spanned two eras. He sprang from one era and took his words and works with him, and reshaped them to suit the new era, just as he had come from Hungary to America, and reshaped and reinvented himself. He was always transforming psychoanalysis. At the end, he was actively engaged in research and exploration into new directions to take psychoanalysis. As Dr. Hardin Branch said, "His influence was nothing short of tremendous."

CHAPTER EIGHT

My grandfather and me

The lives of my grandfather and me were intertwined almost from the beginning of my life. At the time I was born, my grandfather was also in the hospital and recuperating from a heart attack. He would name me after his sister and himself; he would take on the role of father, and make all the important decisions in my life regarding school, residence, friendships, activities, and family matters. He was the only father I had. As he had adored and idolized his father, so too did I idolize him and adore him.

Memories of time spent with my grandfather begin in La Jolla, in the house that sits atop a cliff overlooking the Pacific. When summer arrived in 1945, it was time for my grandparents' annual trek to San Diego. The usual entourage that year expanded to include my mother and me. The trip began in Chicago aboard the Super Chief as it chugged its way through the southwest before arriving at Union Station in Los Angeles. In those days, everyone travelled cross-country by rail. A hired car allowed all of us, and my grandmother's dogs, to get to the beach house. The so-called old route snaked along via the quaint and colorful cities and towns that are now nearly all avoided when driving the interstate. In later years, when making the trip from Los Angeles, I knew that driving past the racetrack at Del Mar and the golf course in

Torrey Pines meant we were close to the end of the journey. Even today I feel excitement as La Jolla gets closer and closer.

The landscape in the front yard was designed by my grandmother, and the house and gardens, the whole property, complemented the natural look of the cliffs overlooking the ocean. Her artistic knowledge and her use of color were put to good use in La Jolla. Chickens were allowed to run free in the enclosed patio as my grandmother thought it important for a young child to have fresh eggs; they were not plentiful in the immediate days after the war. The ocean views were spectacular, from each and every room, and the sun shone brightly on this house, all the time, at least in my memories. This house, and La Jolla, to this day remains for me a beacon of good times and happiness for all. After all, it is the house in which I learned to walk and talk, and the house was always full of family.

My mother, Silvia, remarried in 1946; this time to an aeronautical engineer who lived with his father across the street from her parents. His work kept him in the San Diego area and the family lived on Eads Avenue for several years before his job required a move to Los Angeles. I began school at the La Jolla Country Day School and made friends with a young French girl, Marguerite. When my half-sister was born in 1948, my mother chose my friend's name for her daughter, but altered it a bit to sound more Southern Californian. Marguerite became Marguerita.

My own memory development seems to be sporadic; my first consistent and ongoing memories of my grandfather begin in 1950. The family moved to what is now the border between Century City and Beverly Hills, into a Spanish three bedroom house on Kerwood Avenue. The house had a large greenhouse for orchids and roses that were used to supply the rose garden outside the formal dining room with lovely bushes. The front patio, typical of a Southern California Spanish house, had a fish pond that was visible from the floor-to-ceiling windows in the parlor. At that time Beverly Hills was a sleepy and quiet little village and had an intimate feel to it, like La Jolla. There was the shop where one went for the first party dress, the best shop for toys, the best restaurant for a first date, and so on and so on. I was enrolled in the Overland Elementary School on Ashby Street and my mother often drove me to school in royal fashion in her new car. The Packard was a gift from my grandfather and was previously owned by Carole Lombard and Clark Gable. My mother inherited her love of cars from her mother, my grandmother, as did I. The car was dark in colour, perhaps black or navy blue, with wide whitewall tires and a rumble seat. My mother would pack three or four of my neighborhood chums in the rumble seat and take us for a drive up and down Beverly Glen Blvd. or along little Santa Monica Blvd. past the fountains at the intersection of Wilshire Blvd. A third daughter, Pennie, was born in June 1950.

In 1951 my mother's second marriage became unworkable and she divorced my stepfather who had legally adopted me. My mother and I moved into a small apartment in Westwood Village on Levering Drive, near the UCLA campus. My "Thomas father" obtained custody of my half-sisters Marguerita and Pennie though he told them that he always wanted custody of the three of us. He raised them alone and from that day forward, I was raised as an only child and was considered to be the only grandchild too. I always considered myself an only child. The reasoning behind those decisions will never be known.

Soon after my mother and I moved out of the house on Kerwood, my grandparents came from Chicago to visit, no doubt to check on us. They usually stayed at the Hotel Bel Air located on Stone Canyon Drive and nestled among the gentle hills near UCLA with lush gardens and ponds with white swans. This is where I learned how to swim. The lifeguard at the pool took the time to show me several swimming strokes and being in the pool seemed to come naturally. In later years my grandfather would have to beg me to get out of the pool in Palm Springs. Having my grandparents and my mother around was delightful. Everyone had a good time; there was lots of laughter, and for a six year old, it was thrilling to eat poolside. Another time they visited and stayed at the Holiday House in Malibu. It seems that my grandparents knew all the fun spots to eat and a favorite was the Sea Lion Restaurant in Malibu with its large windows, overlooking the ocean, that were sprayed with water at high tide. California sea lions frolicked in a large pool amid rocks in the front of the restaurant. I remember walking up and down the beach, hand in hand with my grandfather, as we searched for sand dollars and starfish. He loved the sun and was darkly tanned, as was the custom in those days. He had a plethora of Hawaiian-print sport shirts he wore with slacks and, sometimes, Bermuda shorts, but only in California.

My grandfather placed me in a boarding school at the age of seven. He chose Chadwick School in Palos Verdes, then a sprawling sparsely populated community surrounded by horse farms and wide open spaces. Chadwick was and is, according to its website, "… dedicated to academic excellence and to the development of self-confident individuals of exemplary character. Honesty, respect, responsibility, fairness, and compassion, Chadwick's core values, are fostered and modelled in classrooms and co-curricular activities." Chadwick School was founded in 1935 by visionary educator Margaret Lee Chadwick and her husband, a former naval officer lovingly called The Commander by the students, and sits atop another important hill, at least in my memory, this one on the Palos Verdes Peninsula. The Chadwicks believed that a more rural setting was conducive to better educational outcomes and an all-important feeling of security for the children. This school's ideals and goals mirrored those of the Beaver Country Day School, Girl's Latin, and Francis Parker where my mother and aunt were students decades earlier. A progressive educational experience would be offered along with a healthy environment away from the distractions of the hustle and bustle found in the city.

It was hoped that the essential elements of Alexander's growing up in Budapest would be mine as well: stability, order, and consistency. His hopes would be realized. A highlight of the school year was always his visits. He brought me watches from Geneva, toys from the world-famous Uncle Bernie's Toy Menagerie on Rodeo Drive in Beverly Hills with the lemonade tree, and clothes from Saks Fifth Avenue. I remember his visits with fondness even now and I was filled with gleeful anticipation before his car drove up the long winding road to the dorm at Chadwick.

Big Papa and me in Malibu.

During the time when I was in the fourth and fifth grades, and visiting my grandfather, sometimes he would let me carry his briefcase. I was so short, as were my arms, that the briefcase almost skimmed the floor. On other occasions, I would wear his suit jacket. That, too, would almost touch the floor. He was always ready to engage in a small game with me. He seemed to delight in my childhood nonsensical ways. I was happy and felt important when with him.

Most of my classmates at Chadwick boarded and despite seemingly large age differences, all of us were good friends. It was as if the experience created a bond that superseded age. I was friends with the children of Hoagy Carmichael, Robert Walker Sr., the Andrews Sisters, Joan Crawford, Susan Hayward, Ronald Reagan and Jane Wyman, and other celebrities too. Susan Hayward's son Greg Barker was my first boyfriend when we were in the seventh grade. We were class officers as well. I recall she had just won the Oscar for *I Want to Live* and we were all very excited that her twin sons were coming into our class. My maypole dancing partner was Rocky Brynner, the son of actor Yul. Dean Martin's children were there, too, as well as the daughters of Brian Donlevy and Art Linkletter. It was as if we were all placed there, away from home, to get a solid foundation while not being in the way of our parents. I also made friends with teachers and mentors and recall with fondness washing a dorm mother's car as I was fascinated with cars by the fifth grade. My love of cars was no doubt inherited from my grandmother and my mother. I remember John, the cook at the school, who made special cinnamon rolls on the weekends. He often took some of us to the top of the hill where we could see the beaches of Redondo and Manhattan below. Sometimes we went to the beach and saw the early surfers atop large, thick boards. Or, we ventured to the riding club at Portuguese Bend for lessons. These hills are now covered with houses but they were once vacant rolling hills.

That close-knit community played the role of mother and father to me and at the end of those boarding school years, when I returned to live with my mother, my grandfather played the role of father but in a more intimate manner as we then lived together. Chadwick and my grandfather provided me the structure and guidance I needed to succeed in a profession and in personal relationships. I think my grandfather realized my mother's limitations and he arranged for the boarding school. I am forever in his debt for this decision and the positive outcome it provided me. Not all his choices for me were positive. But I believe they were made because he loved me deeply, saw potential in me, and wanted to make sure I succeeded.

In 1957 my mother's third marriage (of five) disintegrated and it seemed an opportune time for my grandfather to suggest we share a residence. He would bear the financial responsibility of running the household and provide security for all of us. I was then a teenager and my mother was in the midst of emotional instability after her marital breakup. Since coming to Los Angeles a year before, my grandfather had taken an apartment on Wilshire Blvd. midway between Westwood Village and Beverly Hills, less than a fifteen-minute drive from the hospital. He searched for and found a larger and more appropriate place for us to live. My grandmother was living in a newly built home in Palm Springs and the La Jolla house had been sold. My grandmother was unable to live in La Jolla permanently as the dampness of the sea air caused arthritic pain that impaired her ability to paint and sculpt. The dryness of the desert better suited her physical needs at the time. The Alexanders would, for the first time since the final days of World War I, live apart from one another and spend long weekends together in Palm Springs.

Our new home was in Westwood Village, near the intersection of Wilshire and Westwood Blvds., not far from the Crest Theatre, the futuristic-looking Ship's Coffee Shop, and the popular Truman's Drive-In. The apartment was a large three bedroom two bath duplex that was Spanish in its exterior design. Some of the furniture in the apartment came from the La Jolla house and from the Chicago house as well. My mother and I shared a bedroom with twin beds. One bedroom, with a separate entrance, became an office for Big Papa where he saw patients mornings and evenings. I would often watch *American Bandstand* after school and had to make sure to leave the room intact and on time before patients arrived. Occasionally I saw some of the patients coming into the home as they often had to wait for him in the parlor. I recognized many as actors from TV or the movies, but I knew I was unable to share that information with my high school friends.

My aunt Kiki said of her own father that he did not know what to do with children and often complained to cousins about her difficult childhood. It was completely different for me, years later when he assumed the role of father. He was attentive, interested, and spent a lot of time with me. Sometimes we went to the Racquet Club for lunch and to play tennis. One of my favorite pastimes was to spend time with him on the golf course, in Palm Springs, and with his cronies after the course was completed. I remember he often played golf with Danny Kaye, and his daughter Dena became my friend for some time when we were both in high school. My grandfather would let me drive the golf cart and then he would squeal in make-believe fear when I drove, along the path, and over a bridge. His mocked fear would bring me to laughter as I continued the drive.

We did not have live-in help at the time, but life was easy and there were some signs of opulence from the past life in Budapest. Food was delivered from a gourmet grocery store, Jurgenson's, and the laundry was picked up and returned in the traditional blue paper with twine. It all seemed to be working out well, for all of us. We always had dinner together and it was a happy time. My grandfather would ask my mother, at 4:00pm or later, if we could have a New England boiled dinner that night. She would be exasperated as it seemed he was not aware of the time involved for such a meal. When we did not eat at home, we ate out. It seems to me that we ate out quite often. One of my grandfather's favorites was an Italian restaurant on Melrose called Chianti. In those days it took about thirty minutes or more to make the drive and I thought it was a long way to go "just to eat." I now understand how one has favorite spots for dinner and is willing to drive. My grandfather disliked eating alone and we often went to The Luau or Ah Fongs in Beverly Hills, the restaurants on the La Cienega strip, Scandia, and Canter's, or to the Polo Lounge at the Beverly Hills Hotel. One of my favorite spots was the Brown Derby where I would order their famous Cobb salad. I do not remember ever eating anything casual with him like a hamburger, a sandwich, or a pizza. For those treats, I went with friends to the Hamburger Hamlet or Mario's, located close to the Fox Village Theatre and the Bruin Theatre. Sometimes I was sent to the market to purchase food for dinner. Minced or ground hamburger meat was never purchased as it was reserved for my grandmother's dogs, as was round steak. Sardines and mackerel were also served to the dogs. We ate three- or four-course meals in the standard European manner and the main course was always followed by a fancy pastry dessert such as an éclair, a Hungarian or Austrian torte, or a Napoleon. There was always a cheese course too. We would sometimes take a short walk and go for a hot fudge sundae at Wil Wright's Ice Cream Parlor. My grandfather enjoyed a Dubonnet before supper and some of his Hungarian Tokay or Palinka afterwards. Palinka, a centuries-old fruit brandy, was once enjoyed at the start of the day and is considered medicine or remedy by many to this day. His choice of Palinka was most often peach or apricot and, not surprisingly, that is the only Hungarian word he taught me … *barack* for peach or apricot. Hungarians love peaches and apricots.

Though his clothes were made by the best tailors, and his shirts came from the best stores, his lapels and the front of his suit jackets were always smudged with cigarette ashes. He was often spotted, in his office, walking on the street, riding in his car, or at home with a cigarette dangling from the corner of his mouth. In fact, one of the photographs of him, gracing the entrance walls to the Chicago Institute for Psycho-analysis, shows him with a cigarette in his mouth. In those days the dangers of smoking were not fully understood and smoking had been glamorized in the movies. He often tried to wipe the ashes from his jacket with his fingertips in a casual flipping motion. It always seemed incongruous for him to walk around with a dull ash mark as he was such a meticulous man in most other ways.

He loved to travel; he loved cameras and taking photographs. He had the newest and best cameras and he often had at least one camera slung around his neck. I remember the minuscule photos from the Minox cameras. He had Leicas and Minoltas. He had lots of fun with his Polaroids. It seems there were always black and white or Kodachrome color slides on top of his bureau. The Nikons and the other single lens reflex cameras had the requisite Zeiss lens. He fancied Swiss gold watches and bought himself new ones each year during the summer trips to Europe. He started to gift me with expensive watches and cameras when I was in the third grade. My love of photography began at that time. He was generous with everyone he loved.

He was an avid reader and his tastes were varied. For nighttime reading he loved mystery novels and his favorite series for a time was Perry Mason by Erle Stanley Gardner. (He would later move on to the James Bond series by Ian Fleming.) He often left his unfinished book on the night stand, to await his return, and I would lie in his bed and read it when he was in Palm Springs. He loved the opera and symphony as well as the gypsy music that reminded him of his beloved Hungary. He loved to go to the movies. At Christmastime he made Liptauer cheese, with poppy seeds and lots of Hungarian paprika, and we hung marzipan wrapped in fancy, shiny paper on the Christmas tree. We lit the traditional candle lights and someone cautiously stood close with a fire

Dr. Franz Alexander on veranda of Palm Springs house.

extinguisher. There were never any mishaps. On Christmas Eve we ate pureed chestnuts warmed in the oven with *schlagsahne* (whipped cream) on top before heading out to friends for a traditional fish dinner followed by midnight mass. I continue these Christmas traditions in my own home. It is another way to keep a connection to the past and to him.

What I did not know was that my grandfather was critical of my mother's parenting and she did not like the scrutiny. He must have been very discreet with his observations or spoken to her only when I was not home. All I knew was that my mother was unhappy with me. I could often hear her, complaining about me to her friends, when I was sitting in the other room. I felt unloved and unwanted by her and that no matter what I did, I was unable to please her.

As deftly as the decision had been made for the three of us to move in together, so, too, was the decision made to separate. My mother summarily ended the living arrangement with my grandfather and behaved like a rebellious teenager and petulant child. If she could not have her own way, there would be no compromise or discussion. She was unable to tolerate either discord or disappointment from others. She merely walked away and this was one such example. It is almost as if her development was stunted at an early age and she was unable to move past that stage.

The change in where we would live was not discussed with me nor was I made aware of problems or disagreements between them. All of a sudden, we were apart and the attention and security I felt with my grandfather was gone. He moved into a suite at the Chateau Marmont situated in West Hollywood. The hotel was built in 1927 and was modelled loosely after the Château d'Amboise in the Loire Valley. When the Chateau Marmont opened it was considered one of the area's most exclusive hotels and offered suites as well as bungalows. As my grandfather got situated in a new living arrangement, my mother and I moved to a smaller apartment; this was during my senior year at University High School. His being apart from me meant that in order to see each other, it had to be done in tandem with my mother or a prearranged solo visit after he finished seeing patients. We often shared a meal at a favorite steak house near Mt. Sinai Hospital.

Whenever we had dinner together he would insist I speak German. He spoke at least four or five languages and felt I should too. Often in the summer months I attended the Berlitz School for language development instead of just hanging out with friends. When we had dinner together he often would say, "Don't speak so fast. Do not slur your words." His words ring in my ears from time to time when I am excited and I remember his caveat; slow down so that others can understand you. His time with me was special and it is, perhaps, that he had time then. He was undoubtedly comfortable about his contributions to psychoanalysis and could concentrate more on family. Or maybe he was making up for lost time with his own children with a granddaughter who had no father. When we dined together he would bring me home. Sometimes his chauffeur would drive the car, his Chrysler New Yorker, in those days nicknamed "the doctor's car." My grandfather was a notoriously bad driver.

For the final three years of his life I saw my grandfather on a regular basis. I would either go to Palm Springs with him on the weekends, or I would see him in the city. If I spent a weekend in Palm Springs, we swam together or he took me along with him to the golf course. My grandmother taught classes at the summer institute run by the University of Southern California in Idyllwild known as the Idyllwild School of Music and the Arts (ISOMATA). The ISOMATA was founded by Dr. Max Krone and his wife, who dreamed of a rural area where people from different backgrounds could come together and engage in the arts. They chose for their school the mountains above the desert town of Palm Springs. A large house was rented for the entire summer and my grandfather would spend the weekdays in Los Angeles and join my grandmother every Thursday night. I would spend the weekends there, atop the mountain, and enjoy the casualness of this small mountain village summer retreat that was cooler than the desert floor below. The three of us would cook together to prepare the meals, sit outside and read to each other, and do crossword puzzles. In the evenings we listened to the radio shows from Europe on the Grundig short-wave radio.

As I grew into my late teens, Big Papa inspired me to seek academic excellence, to commit myself to public service when I chose a career in clinical social work; he taught me to seek answers, and to think for myself. He was the epitome of an educated intellectual who had a strong social conscience as well. He wanted to bring about positive change to his field. He encouraged independence and sharing what you had with those who had less. I do recall that he never became impatient with me nor did he become angry or lecture me. I do know that he was often impatient with minor details and preferred to focus on the larger picture of an issue. I am like him in that way. He was always kind, compassionate, interested, and engaged with whatever I wanted to share with him. He always made me feel special and loved, and his dark brown eyes seemed to twinkle when he saw me. He was my teacher, my father, my pal, and confidant. And I needed all those in my life.

I was nineteen when my grandfather died. I had seen him a few days earlier, for dinner, as was the usual custom between us. It was a most difficult time for me and still, all these years later, memories of that time right after his death brings sadness. I still miss him. People say that pain eases as the years pass and that "it will get better." We all know, as we grow older, that is not true. The only change is that we do not experience the pain as often when we do not remember our lost loved one daily. When I think of my grandfather and his importance in my life, personally and professionally, I am filled with love, gratitude, and sadness. The love he felt for me was pure and kind. He taught me everything I would need in later life. I feel gratitude for his realization of my childhood needs and his decision to take a primary role and to meet those needs. I am, nonetheless, still sad, as I was at nineteen, that many others had more years with him than I did. He always seemed so young and vibrant. I, like others, was shocked when he died. Along with the rest of the psychoanalytic community, I thought he would live forever.

The feelings I had for my grandfather have vacillated from near idol worship when I was a teenager to disillusionment, sadness, and confusion as I uncovered family secrets and the ways in which he deliberately kept my family, his family, from me and me from them. When I consider how his decisions shaped my life, his life, my choices, and my development, I am profoundly sad. I wish he were here so I could ask: Why did you keep me from your family? Why did you really change my name? Why did you not help your sister in Budapest more after World War II? Why had I never heard of Borbala? When my cousin Vera sat at your Thanksgiving table, why did she not know of me? Why was my mother's second marriage made to look like a first wedding? Why do so many of my cousins say, "We did not know where your mother was, nobody knew," when you knew all along? Were you so ashamed of her and her rebellious behaviour that you needed to keep us away from the rest of the family? Did you consider the consequences at the time or were you merely trying to clean up your daughter's mistakes in order to make yourself look better to your world? It is almost impossible for me to comprehend his aversion to my father, a most intelligent man who would study chemistry and physics and become a nuclear physicist and earn many accolades during the course of a distinguished career. This is the man who remained in love and in contact with my mother for his entire life.

Both sets of my grandparents did the same thing. They had all come to America, left behind their lives and family in Europe, and reinvented themselves through hard work, education, and opportunity. Their generation may well be the last that could come across the ocean and emerge as brand new on the other side. There was opportunity for change and few ways for secrets and lies to be uncovered. Though all the Alexander children had the opportunity to succeed financially and in careers, none found the success my grandfather did. His success made him the star of the family and he revelled in its light.

Colleagues say he was adored by his younger brother Paul and younger sisters Borka and Lilla and was close to all his siblings. However, when his sister, having lost everything in post-World War II Budapest, wrote to him for financial assistance, he sent $80 and a food package. It is almost impossible for me to make sense of it all especially since this man, my grandfather, grew up in a tight-knit family with very traditional values that undoubtedly included commitment to family. Maybe he was trying to protect her? Maybe she only asked for a small sum?

He was, most assuredly, a man of contradictions. I believe he was more fragile and insecure than anyone thought. On the outside he was magnetic and energetic. He exuded confidence and grace. He was a busy man who loved work, and he loved the challenges of new ideas, and putting them into practice. When he died his desk in Palm Springs was littered and full of manuscripts and other papers he was working on at the time. His zest for life and his enthusiasm often made him appear younger to his students, colleagues, and to his family. His death, at seventy-three, was therefore a shock to many. More than one has said his death was sudden and early.

He was reluctant to share himself with others yet craved attention and the spotlight almost as if in a superficial way. He was a perfect host and enjoyed having people in his home. His nieces and nephews, cousins I have come to know in the past four years, say he was accustomed to and loved the limelight and was treated by the rest of the family as a celebrity. His achievements were held up to the others as an ideal of what can happen with hard work and talent. He enjoyed the glitz and glamour of being the most prominent American psychoanalyst of his time and the founder of the Chicago Institute. Despite growing up in a close-knit family, he was not what we would call close to his siblings or his children. His youngest daughter was so distraught by her upbringing that she entered analysis with Dr. Albrecht Meyer for many years. Eventually Dr. Meyer said she did not need analysis, she needed a mother. Dr. Hedda Bolgar stepped in and assumed the role of close friend and surrogate mother.

However distant he may have appeared to his children, he was not that way with me. I think that our special relationship was forged in order to make amends for the poor relationship he had with his children, both in their younger years and in adulthood. I think he was living in the new world with old world traditions and those role expectations still prominent in his mind. He was unable to show Silvia and Kiki the love and attention they needed. He was the center of the home in that all decisions revolved around him yet his physical presence was rarely felt. He appeared open, but was really a rather private man. It must have been painful for him to watch his oldest child flounder in relationships and be unable, despite her intelligence, to focus on an appropriate career and become totally independent. He always found it easy to make a commitment and follow through; my mother was one who rarely finished anything and whose relationships, too, were superficial and short-lived. He was, as he often admitted, confused regarding his children.

Silvia's poor choices and an inability to follow his footsteps in a medical or scientific career may have been predetermined by family discussions and expectations. My mother had been my grandfather's perfect daughter, a pretty woman who looked like her petite and blonde Italian mother. It is said that once my grandmother said to my mother, "You are pretty. Men will take care of you." The message was clear: You are not really expected to make a name for yourself. You can be a decoration. My mother did attend Mills College in the Bay area for one year before transferring in the fall of 1940 to the University of Wisconsin in Madison. She would complete just two years of university before returning to Chicago and, again, moving in with her parents and seeking employment at the University of Chicago when World War II broke out. In contrast, my grandparents said to my aunt, who was not as finely boned, and more of a tomboy, "You must study and learn to be independent. That is something nobody can take away from you." It was assumed she would study and follow a career path; it was just for her to decide which area of interest. She originally chose English and went to the University of Chicago where she obtained an undergraduate degree and a master's degree. Eventually she obtained her doctorate from the University of Southern California in social psychology. Though she often claimed she wanted her own identity, apart from her father, she signed her personal cheques "Dr. F. Alexander."

He was an academic who was forward thinking in his theories yet clung with tenacity to traditions familiar to him from his past. He was organized in his thinking, in the midst of writing two new books, but when he died, his papers were in disarray and there was no will. Because of this, a family friend, Morton Phillips, executor of Alexander's estate and the husband of Pauline Phillips, better known as Dear Abby, was forced to turn over all his papers to his widow, my grandmother. My grandmother, in her angst and grief, put all his important papers and books in huge Bekins moving crates and left them for years. When she began to exhibit symptoms of dementia, my aunt Kiki was granted conservatorship and saved the papers, returned them to the Chicago Institute but then reclaimed them in the early 1990s. Just prior to her death in 1992, she gave the papers to Dr. George Pollock who had hoped to write a biography of Alexander. Unfortunately Dr. Pollock died before he was able to write the biography and his heirs have donated the papers to Cornell University.

Big Papa died on the morning of Sunday March 8, 1964 at his home in Palm Springs. He had not been feeling well for several days and told his colleague and long-time friend Hedda Bolgar. She insisted he not go swimming with a viral infection and he called her Saturday March 7, 1964 to let her know he was feeling better and had followed her instructions about not going into the pool. It is thought he died of pneumonia though a post mortem was not done.

The days immediately after his death are a blur as we travelled from Pacific Palisades to Palm Springs. My aunt ran every stop light and stop sign during the journey that began just after 7:00 that morning. Friends and colleagues from all over the world, the Who's Who in Psychiatry and Psychoanalysis, attended the funeral mass at St. Theresa's Catholic Church in Palm Springs. The church was, as they say, filled to the rafters. My grandfather was buried in the Holy Cross Catholic Cemetery in San Diego, close to his beloved La Jolla home and the part of the world he enjoyed so much. I believe La Jolla is where he was the happiest, that is, besides his younger years spent in Budapest. After the funeral, a week later, I met my father. He had promised my grandfather decades before that he would stay out of my life. He waited until my grandfather died to make his entrance.

All of those emotions from long ago have come flooding back as I journey back, into the past, and through my grandfather's life. Writing this book, about his life, his family, and mine, too, his accomplishments, and his challenges, makes me realize I still miss him. The overwhelming feeling now for me is immense gratitude. He was indeed my idol, my Big Papa. He was and will always be the most important person in my life. I believe his place in history is secure, too. He was an innovator, a teacher, an educator, and a man who challenged others' ideas and their thinking. He was intensely curious and wanted to share that with others. He was a prolific writer in a language that was not his mother tongue, English. He was scholarly without being pedantic. He was fun loving without being comical. He loved his family and friends and enjoyed spending time with them. He pushed boundaries among his more traditional colleagues and that was his inner essence, to always seek new ideas for betterment. He was, indeed, a pioneer in the field of psychoanalysis whose ideas are relevant today. He was always reaching for the ideal, for the stars. He was his father's son and the father would have been proud. He is a man who made mistakes from which we continue to grow and learn today.

He held the key to open Pandora's box. His legacy to me is my past and my future. He helped me bring the family back together again.

He will always be my Big Papa. My version of his Sun King.

The family today

Now it is 2015, and more than 150 years have slipped by since my great grandfather Bernard Alexander was born in a little Hungarian town near Budapest. The descendants of his wife's father and uncle, Judah and Pinkus Broessler, came together twice for family reunions, once in La Jolla (2011), and a second time we travelled together from Vienna to Uhersky Brod in the Czech Republic, on to Budapest and back to Vienna (2012). As family was at long last revealed to me over the last four years, I am still trying to get answers to the question of WHY? I may never know all the answers. What I do know is that I am no longer the lost child, named for the other one who was lost after dying in a scalding accident. My cousin Robin echoed my feelings recently and said he felt like a lost child as his father and mother told him nothing of the Alexander family either. Most who attended the reunions thought they had no family. The keeping of secrets was a shared behavior among various family members.

I am no longer on the outside looking in, like the little match girl, with her nose pressed against the window. I am included. I belong somewhere. I have family, I have roots. I have connections to the past, and share physical and personality traits with others. I am high-strung and obsessive, like my family. I share a love of cooking, like my family.

I can be anxious, like my family. How good that sounds ... like my family. And an important part of my story, and theirs, is that we are Jewish. I may never find the answers, but now instead of anger and confusion, I feel compassion and curiosity. And I do not feel the need to hide any more.

I think that Franz Alexander's legacy was his commitment to research, his progressive ideas about the practice of psychoanalysis, be they a shortened period of analysis, lay analysts, or the corrective emotional experience. His legacy also includes his writings and work in psycho-dynamic psychotherapy, and his founding principles of psychosomatic medicine. One of his greatest legacies, however, may be our family and the stories of those from his family who influenced him. Those stories and those people allow us all greater insight into the man and his many accomplishments. These accomplishments still stand today, even after the controversy and criticism of years long ago, and help to make him, as Martin Grotjahn said, a "pioneer of psychoanalysis." It is said that it is impossible to know where you are going until you know where you have been. This holds true in psychoanalysis as well as in life.

AFTERWORD

Dr. Carl Bell

Why does someone write a biography of a great man? Is it the motivation of a doting granddaughter or is it something more? In this book we have a little of the first and a lot of the latter, specifically, a personal story about a man who had curiosity, conviction, and courage. A physician who was not afraid to journey to unknown vistas while seeking to create an understanding of the greatest mystery of all—that of the human mind and how it relates to the body. This is the biography of the world-renowned psychiatrist Dr. Franz Alexander, MD, told by his granddaughter—Ilonka Venier Alexander. Ilonka Alexander has given psychiatry, medicine, and the world a great gift— an up close and personal biography of her grandfather—the father of psychosomatic medicine.

As I read the biography and looked at the photos, it struck me that the members of Franz Alexander's family looked like aristocrats and they had the "chops" to prove it. When I mentioned this to Ilonka, she did admit that her grandmother was a descendent from the doges in Venice. I also commented to her that I am convinced that the immigrants are the very people that have made America strong, and she replied, "We all came from somewhere." Learning that the Alexander family had begun in Budapest and were of Jewish descent, but had sought to convert to Catholicism, reminded me of the difficulty Jews had in sixteenth-century Spain and how Teresa of Avila was of Jewish descent and yet was canonized a Catholic saint by Pope Gregory XV (Clissold, 1977). Therefore, it would seem—no matter how things change they often stay the same.

The information about Franz Alexander's father—Bernard Alexander (a scholar in his own right) is captivating. Dr. Alexander's father, who was also the editor of the *Journal of Philosophy*, asked his son to write a review of Freud's *The Interpretation of Dreams*. It is intriguing that both father and son thought it did not make any sense. Accordingly, this personal family biography highlights the confusion, the twists and turns of life that are so mesmerizing. The description of the family's time in the last days of the nineteenth century in Budapest is compelling.

Ilonka Alexander writes so beautifully and poignantly that I found myself transported to a place and time I have never been. I found myself imagining what it must have been like for Franz Alexander to be at the "cutting edge" of psychiatry and psychoanalysis and to "hang out" with Sigmund Freud, and to be the first student at the Berlin Psychoanalytic Institute having survived the ravages of World War I. Surely, this was quite an adventure and not for the faint of heart.

The stories of the other Alexander children born into Franz's family are fascinating. As in any family there was the tragedy of Little Ilonka; and there were successes—Erzsebet the opera singer; Magdalena an art historian who wrote several books; Borbala who may have been too Jewish for the family to embrace; Paul who invented techniques for evaporating metals in ultra-high vacuums so they could coat objects; and Lillian who was an actress in Hungarian, French, and German venues. Thus, this well written biography of Franz Alexander highlights the multifarious paths that families can take in life and illustrates how high standards of sophistication and scholarship can be transmitted through generations. There are equally interesting side stories of Dr. Alexander's siblings' children and their wide-ranging paths toward success in life.

The chapter on Dr. Alexander's time in Berlin after World War I is enthralling and anyone familiar with the history of the formation of psychoanalysis will be charmed by the iteration of the beginning of the Berlin Psychoanalytic Institute. Having been familiar with Karl Abraham's work on the relationship of sexual trauma to the etiology of neurosis and psychosis, it was interesting for me to learn that Dr. Abraham was a mentor of Dr. Alexander. The descriptions of "infighting" are likely familiar to every academician, and we learn how the protocols of analysis had not been formally laid down, resulting in a great deal of creativity in analyst and analysand relationships. Ilonka's description that "everything was pretty made up as they went along," reminded me of one lengthy conversation I had with Dr. Roy Grinker, Sr. He beautifully described for me the analysis that he received from Sigmund Freud and the walks they used to take, the lunches they shared, and how Jo-Fi (Freud's dog) would interrupt his analysis with Freud and Dr. Freud would joke that "Herr Grinker" was producing good associations as Jo-Fi had sought entry to their session. Of course, when Jo-Fi would scratch the door to go back into Freud's apartment, Dr. Freud would tell "Herr Grinker" that he was resisting.

Ilonka Alexander mentions Freud's minimal expectations for change in therapy (antithetical to her grandfather's hopeful expectations of analysis), and that reminded me of my favourite Freud quote: "Ethics are remote from me ... I do not break my head very much about good and evil, but I have found little that is 'good' about human beings on the whole. In my experience most of them are trash, no matter whether they publicly subscribe to this or that ethical doctrine or to none at all ... If we are to talk of ethics, I subscribe to a high ideal from which most of the human beings I have come across depart most lamentably" (Roazen, 1975, p. 146). My suspicion is that Freud saw in Dr. Alexander someone who subscribed to his ethics and thus said, "All of us count on you as one of our strongest hopes for the future." My sense is this quote reflects Freud's observation that most people do not make an investment in themselves and do not challenge themselves as both Freud and Alexander had done in trying to help people understand the truth of themselves; accordingly, Freud's notion that most people are trash—harsh but real. It takes a great deal to be honest with one's self—intrapsychic courage is hard to come by.

Another fascinating little-known Alexander factoid (at least by me) was his interest in criminal personalities. I had not known that William Healy, the first director of the Institute for Juvenile Research (IJR) (birthplace of child psychiatry—see Schowalter, 2000, p. 463) had gone to Berlin to discuss a book on criminal psychology Herr Professor had written. We later learn that Drs. Alexander and Healy collaborated on the psychoanalytic study of delinquency which was a cornerstone of

IJR in its earlier days. This emphasis was on support of the mission of the first juvenile court started in Chicago by Nobel winning social worker Jane Addams in 1899. I suspect this had something to do with Dr. Alexander's eventually heading IJR which Dr. Healy first directed in 1909 when it began—I was shocked to learn that Dr. Franz Alexander and I had both been the directors of the Institute of Juvenile Research. I had also not known of Karl Menninger's relationship to Dr. Alexander, but when I was in psychiatric residency in Chicago, I seem to recall hearing about train trips from Topeka to Chicago for analytic sessions. It is interesting how in each geographic area of psychiatric thought in the US there is a rich history that we seldom appreciate until a biography like this comes along.

Having grown up in Hyde Park in Chicago, and interacting with the Chicago Institute for Psychoanalysis, I find this book holds many related memories for me. I recall a memory of when I presented a narcissistic patient to Karl Menninger (apparently Dr. Alexander's colleague): he was pretty rough on me despite my carefully reading his *Theory of Psychoanalytic Technique* (Menninger, 1958). He had some misgivings about having written it because of his perception that his suggestions were being used to treat patients with narcissistic personality disorders, and he did not feel that was appropriate due to their less developed psyches (of course this did not prevent me from having him sign his book).

Also, having had some dealings with the Chicago Institute for Psychoanalysis, knowing George Pollock, and Jerome Winer, all of whom are mentioned in the book, I found the chapter on "Chicago and the Time of His Life" very engaging. I was shocked to learn that Heinz Kohut (who many in Chicago feel was the second coming of Freud—he tackled the issue of narcissism which Freud did not spend a whole lot of time addressing), who I corresponded with a few times about the relationship between narcissism and racism, had also distanced himself from his Jewish heritage. You would think society has progressed to the point of more acceptance and less of a need to disown one's heritage whatever its supposed caste. I guess the individual human tendency toward narcissism and its scaffolding of in-group and out-group behavior has not changed and likely will not change despite our enlightened wish that such silliness would vanish and a "live, let live" notion could take firm hold. Moreover, this biography illustrates that psychiatrists are people too.

I recall reading Dr. Alexander's book on *Psychosomatic Medicine*, when I was in my psychiatric residency and being fascinated by his psychosomatic observations about "expressive innervations" (Alexander, 1950, pp. 56–58). He noted that when the mind is in an emotional state, the expression of this emotional state is observed in the person's breathing. For example, deep sighing respiration is seen in depression, shallow panting respiration is seen in panic, breath holding is seen in concentration, irregular breathing is seen in distress, and a short, quick, deep inspiration is seen in surprise. Having been an explorer into my inner being, this observation by a psychoanalyst of Alexander's caliber suggested he observed how individuals' mental states influence their breathing patterns. In Eastern culture there is a strong belief and empirical observation that the breathing patterns can have an influence on the person's mental state. Thus, by learning to train and control the breath an individual is able to observe and control his reaction to his thoughts and emotions. Long and calm breathing creates a steady, calm mind, and vice versa.

His granddaughter, the author, notes that Dr. Alexander "insisted he concentrated his efforts on practice, not theory." Unfortunately, this pioneer of psychosomatic medicine did not have sophisticated technology, currently available to us in the late twentieth and early twenty-first centuries. Such new technology has allowed recent scientists like Dr. Steve Porges to disentangle that complex physiology of the vagus nerve and to explicate *The Polyvagal Theory* (2011). Yet, it is engrossing to understand how Dr. Alexander's empirical clinical observations are often borne out by strict scientific research. So, for example, despite this lack of refined equipment being available to him, Dr. Alexander's observations of the emotional factors in cardiovascular disturbances still ring true and have been confirmed by the more advanced research in Chesney and Rosenman's edited book—*Anger and Hostility in Cardiovascular and Behavioral Disorders* (1985).

From Ilonka's description of the Alexanders' trips to La Jolla, CA, I can imagine Dr. Alexander visiting Hollywood to be with his other European Jewish psychoanalysts who we learn from the biography had a strange attraction to Hollywood. I recall, even before becoming a psychiatrist, the 1945 Alfred Hitchcock film *Spellbound*, produced by David O. Selznick who had a fruitful psychoanalysis and who began the beginning of the film with an infomercial on psychoanalysis.

This wonderful biography also contains some of Dr. Alexander's contributions to the field of psychiatry—the corrective emotional experience, brief treatment, intensive short-term dynamic psychotherapy—all of which I have been enamored with over the past forty-five years. Based on Dr. Alexander's revelation of the corrective emotional experience, when I am mainly prescribing psychotropic medication for patients to keep them out of jail or a psychiatric hospital, I have always figured out what corrective emotional experience they need to right their paths. As Freud noted (1930a, p. 130) in his footnote on Dr. Alexander's *The Psychoanalysis of the Total Personality* (1927)—the two main pathogenic methods of upbringing—over-strictness and spoiling—are the two basic issues I see in my patients. There are those who do not feel loved or who have not experienced empathy—so I try to provide understanding and acceptance; and there are those who are running wild and so I try to provide appropriate need limits. The difficulty is some patients have both dynamics going on and some psychiatrists only want to be the loving parent imago while others try to be the authoritarian imago, and most people need both to self correct.

A biography tells one, if you do not know where you are from, it will be difficult to determine where you are going. I recall my only millionaire friend, Dempsey Travis, telling me that he used to read obituaries and biographies to learn the secrets of a successful life. I think this biography is very telling of Franz Alexander's life and people should know those details from an insider's viewpoint as they put context and feeling into science—this is a good thing. I have been honored to be a part of this work. As we become more and more charmed with biological psychiatry and neuropsychiatry, we must not forget the wisdom that is contained in psychoanalysis: it is not either/or, rather it is both/and. Dr. Alexander and his work exemplified the best of both for his time.

References

Alexander, F. (1927). *The Psychoanalysis of the Total Personality: The Applicability of Freud's Theory of the Ego to the Neuroses.* B. Glueck & B. D. Lewin (Trans.). New York: Nervous and Mental Diseases Publishing, 1930.

Alexander, F. (1950). *Psychosomatic Medicine.* New York: W. W. Norton.

Chesney, M. A., & Rosenman, R. H. (Eds.) (1985). *Anger and Hostility in Cardiovascular and Behavioral Disorders.* Washington, DC: Hemisphere Publishing.

Clissold, S. (1977). *The Wisdom of the Spanish Mystics.* New York: New Directions.

Freud, S. (1930a). *Civilization and Its Discontents. S. E., 21*. London: Hogarth.

Menninger, K. (1958). *Theory of Psychoanalytic Technique*. New York: Harper.

Porges, S. (2011). *The Polyvagal Theory*. New York: W. W. Norton.

Roazen, P. (1975). *Freud and His Followers*. New York: Knopf.

Schowalter, J. E. (2000). Child and adolescent psychiatry comes of age, 1944–1994. In: R. W. Menninger & J. C. Nemiah (Eds.), *American Psychiatry after World War II—1944–1994*. Washington, DC: American Psychiatric Press.

REFERENCES

Alexander, F. (1956a). *Psychoanalysis and Psychotherapy*. New York: W. W. Norton.

Alexander, F. (1956b). Franz Alexander: The man who brought Freud here. *Chicago* magazine, 3: 24–31.

Alexander, F. (1960). *The Western Mind in Transition*. New York: Random House.

Alexander, F. (1964). Presidential address. *The Academy of Psychoanalysis Newsletter*, 7: 1–9.

Alexander, F. (1987). Life with father. In: H. Strean (Ed.), *Growing Up Observed: Tales from Analysts' Children* (pp. 3–17). New York: Haworth Press.

Alexander, F., & Eissler, K. (1954). *Interview with Franz Alexander*. Washington, DC: Library of Congress (unpublished).

Alexander, F., Eisenstein, S., & Grotjahn, M. (Eds.) (1966). *Psychoanalytic Pioneers*. New York: Basic Books.

Alexander, F., & French, T. (1946). *Psychoanalytic Therapy*. New York: Ronald Press.

Alexander, F., & Staub, H. (1956). *The Criminal, the Judge and the Public*. Glencoe, IL: Free Press.

Blumenfield, M., & Strain, J. J. (Eds.) (2006). *Psychosomatic Medicine*. Philadelphia, PA: Lippincott Williams & Wilkins.

Burnham, J. (Ed.) (2012). *After Freud Left: A Century of Psychoanalysis in America*. Chicago, IL: University of Chicago Press.

Casement, P. (1990). *Further Learning from the Patient*. London: Routledge & Kegan Paul.

Cooper, A. (2005). *The Quiet Revolution in American Psychoanalysis*. Hove, UK: Brunner-Routledge.

Eissler, K. R. (1950). The Chicago Institute of Psychoanalysis and the sixth period of the development of psychoanalytic technique. *Journal of General Psychology, 42*: 103–157.

French, T. (1964). In memoriam. *Psychosomatic Medicine, 26*: 203–208.

Gabbard, G. O., & Gabbard, K. (1999). *Psychiatry and the Cinema (2nd edition)*. Arlington, VA: American Psychiatric Publishing.

Gabor, E. (1986). *Bernat Alexander*. Budapest: Akademiai Kiado.

Grosskurth, P. (1991). *Freud's Secret Ring and the Politics of Psychoanalysis*. New York: Addison-Wesley Publishing Co., pp. 20–21.

Grotjahn, M. (1964). Franz Alexander: Teacher, student and pioneer of psychoanalysis. *Journal of Nervous and Mental Disorders, 140*: 319–322.

Kavka, J. (1984). Fifty years of psychoanalysis in Chicago: A historical perspective. In: G. Pollock & J. Gedo (Eds.), *Psychoanalysis: The Vital Issues, Vol. II* (pp. 465–493). New York: International Universities Press.

Kendall, D. (1970). Obituary: Alfred Rényi. *Journal of Applied Probability, 7*: 509–522.

Levenson, D. (1994). *Mind, Body, and Medicine: A History of the American Psychosomatic Society*. McLean, VA: Susan O'Donnell.

Lipsitt, D. (2006). *Psychosomatic Medicine: The History of the New Specialty*. In: M. Blumenfield & J. J. Strain (Eds.), *Psychosomatic Medicine* (pp. 1–20). Philadelphia, PA: Lippincott Williams & Wilkins.

Lukacs, J. (1988). *Budapest 1900: A Historical Portrait of a City and Its Culture*. New York: Weidenfeld & Nicolson.

Lukacs, J. (2013). *A Short History of the Twentieth Century*. Cambridge, MA: Harvard University Press.

McBride, M. (1935). Voice salvaging her career: Hungarian singer has saved many stars for the talkies. *Milwaukee Journal*.

McLean, H. (1965). Franz Alexander: 1891–1964. *International Journal of Psychoanalysis, 46*: 247–250.

Moberly, E. (1985). *The Psychology of Self and Other*. London: Routledge & Kegan Paul.

Pollock, G. (1978). The Chicago Institute for Psychoanalysis from 1932 to the present. In: J. Quen & E. Carlson (Eds.), *American Psychoanalysis: Origins and Development* (pp. 109–126). New York: Brunner/Mazel.

Roazen, Paul (1985). *Helene Deutsch: A Psychoanalyst's Life*. Garden City, New York: Anchor Press/Doubleday.

Rubins, J. (1978). *Karen Horney: Gentle Rebel of Psychoanalysis*. New York: Dial Press.

Saul, L. (1964). Franz Alexander. *Psychoanalytic Quarterly, 33*: 420–423.

Schmidt, E. (2010). The Berlin tradition in Chicago: Franz Alexander and the Chicago Institute for Psychoanalysis. *Psychoanalysis and History, 12*: 69–83.

Terez, V. (2000). *Children of Social Trauma*. London: Jessica Kingsley.

Turán, P. (1976). *The Life of Alfréd Rényi (1921–1970)*. Budapest, Hungary: Akademiai Kiado.

Van Saher, L. (1947). *The Echo*. New York: E.P. Dutton & Co.

Van Saher, L. (1949). *Macamba*. New York: E.P. Dutton & Co.

Van Saher, L. (1964). *Exotic Cookery*. Cleveland & New York: World Publishing Co.

Weissman, E. B. & Moore, G. (2009). *The War Came to Me: A story of endurance and survival*. Lanham, MD: University Press of America.

INDEX

Made in the USA
Middletown, DE
03 August 2023